"*The Moral Premise* is insightful, thought-provoking, and unique. I wish more people were writing the kinds of things Stan is writing. It's a much-needed, fresh approach to the art and craft of writing."
— Ed Solomon, Screenwriter-Director
Levity, Men in Black, Bill and Ted's Excellent Adventure

"Really good stuff! Stan Williams has created a new bible for screenwriters. Should be required reading, retroactively, for every working Hollywood screenwriter, and the primer on which every aspiring new scribe cuts his teeth. Cause and effect... motive behind every action... the apple in Eve's hand... the basic elements in the giant continuing narrative that is the universe."
— Brian Bird, Screenwriter/Producer
Bopha!, Call Me Claus, Touched by an Angel

"*The Moral Premise* — theme, spiritual spine, controlling idea, hidden (universal) truth, emotional through-line, informing vision — call it what you will! All effective stories have it. Williams helps film writers and critics alike understand the heart of a story. Given its strong blend of theory, illustration, and practical suggestion, Williams' book is important reading for screenwriters, filmmakers, and even film critics."
— Robert Johnston, Ph.D., Fuller Theological Seminary;
Co-Director, Reel Spirituality Institute

"A well-argued, well-researched tool (and fuel!) for creating vital screenplays. Stan Williams connects box office success to enduring human virtues. *The Moral Premise* provides a guiding principle to drive you from Fade In to the closing credits."
— Craig Detweiler, Screenwriter/Author: *A Matrix of Meanings*; Chair: Film/TV/Radio, Biola University

"*The Moral Premise* is an elegant explanation for why our best stories are often so much wiser and nobler than are we, the storytellers. I can't help but wonder what the phenomenon Stan Williams so masterfully expounds is trying to tell us about our truest selves."
— Christopher Riley, Screenwriter,
Author of *The Hollywood Standard*

"This is terrific! Stan Williams' book does what an undergrad and graduate education in film could not: distill what makes a movie 'good' into a concise, workable theory that guides every scene. I've read all the major screenwriting texts and their methods are all based on the script containing a solid moral premise. I wish I had this book back in film school. It would have saved me untold hours of agony trying to salvage scripts that had one simple, yet fatal flaw: they lacked a moral premise."
— Jim Rossow, Screenwriter, *Hijacking Hollywood*

THE MORAL PREMISE

HARNESSING VIRTUE & VICE
FOR BOX OFFICE SUCCESS

STANLEY D. WILLIAMS, PH.D.

Published by Michael Wiese Productions
11288 Ventura Blvd., Suite 621
Studio City, CA 91604
tel. (818) 379-8799
fax (818) 986-3408
mw@mwp.com
www.mwp.com

Cover Design: MWP
Book Layout: Gina Mansfield
Editor: Paul Norlen

Printed by McNaughton & Gunn, Inc., Saline, Michigan
Manufactured in the United States of America

Library of Congress Cataloging-in-Publication Data

Williams, Stanley D., 1947-
  The moral premise : harnessing virtue & vice for box office success / Stanley D. Williams.
    p. cm.
  ISBN 1-932907-13-0
  1. Motion pictures--Moral and ethical aspects. 2. Motion picture authorship--Moral and ethical aspects. I. Title.
  PN1995.5.W55 2006
  791.43'653--dc22
                                        2005029095

for

My best friend, first wife, and lover, Pam...
who still lets me do this stuff.

❧

My good friend and writing partner, Bill...
who loves movies and a good story.

CONTENTS

List of Tables

List of Figures

FOREWORD

In this dismal age in which we seem to have thrown away the moral compass, somebody seems to have found it again. I jump up and down in my classes and in Hollywood story meetings about the desperate desire of the audience for entertainment that embodies some moral principles, some guidelines for ethical living, some prescription for a healthier world and a saner life. *The Moral Premise* dares to suggest that movies might actually mean something, that they can be more than the brain candy that passes for amusement today. It brings us back to the vital first principles that used to make the movies an important part of our lives, and I recommend it for all those who want to bring depth and meaning into their writing.

— Christopher Vogler, author of *The Writer's Journey*

PREFACE

This is a book about the Moral Premise and how it is a fundamental part of every successful[1] movie's structure. It is also a book about how you, as one of today's filmmakers, can appropriate the Moral Premise to create great and successful motion pictures.

The heart of this book is about narrative story structure. At first glance, structuring a story for success may sound like just the screenwriter's job. But story structure is also the job of the director and many others. The "director as auteur" is a concept that is not likely to fade away in our lifetime. But the most successful directors know that film is a highly collaborative art; and they work hard to collaborate with their screenwriters, producers, casting agents, actors, directors of photography, production designers, art directors, composers, and distributors. Although I occasionally refer specifically to the screenwriter, this book has been written for filmmakers regardless of what hat they happen to be wearing today.

Furthermore, this book is not restricted to motion pictures. The Moral Premise is a natural part of all successful narrative stories. The Moral Premise was written about by the ancients and it is still a foundational necessity of all stories today, whether those stories are carried on by oral tradition, in print, on the stage, on television, through the Internet... or through whatever else comes along. For now, and for readability, I'll focus on filmmaking.

As a screenwriter, by imbuing a true Moral Premise into your story, you can create multidimensional, motivated characters as you decide what those characters should do, will do, won't do or can't... and in the process save a great deal of time and aggravation.

As a producer, by understanding how a true Moral Premise affects all of the production elements, you can focus your pitch as you attempt to motivate investors, directors, agents, department heads,

---

[1] In this book, the term "successful" and its synonyms generally refer to *relative* domestic box office gross sales when compared to budget, distribution, and marketing expenses. For evaluation of stories told before the invention of box office grosses, the reader will have to substitute other appropriate measures.

editors, and distributors... and in the process advance the schedule and save budget.

As a director, by being aware of how a true Moral Premise can support and inform your vision, you can inspire actors and department heads to physically and emotionally connect with the audience... and in the process save days in planning, setups, and coverage.

As an actor, by contemplating how a true Moral Premise affects your character's arc, you can connect to your character's reality as you internalize motivations... and in the process create an emotionally authentic and fascinating performance.

As a department head, by visualizing the story's true Moral Premise you can enhance the story's telling as you make the myriad creative decisions your discipline demands... and in the process inspire cast, crew, and audiences by underscoring the story's unity.

When those involved in the film's gestation and birth know what the movie is really about, every decision they make becomes more focused, easier, purposeful, and exciting, which, altogether, positions the film for box office success. That is what this book purports to explain and help you do.

Although a number of other screenwriting how-to authors raise the centrality and importance of the Moral Premise concept, this present volume was necessary for several reasons. First, there was a need to clarify and consolidate the different terms that in the past have been used. Second, because the Moral Premise is ubiquitous in all successful stories there was a need for a comprehensive explanation of that connection. Third, for something so important it seemed natural to make available to writers a "how-to" process for ensuring that a true Moral Premise could be at the heart of their stories.

This book is laid out deductively. Part I approaches the Moral Premise academically. Chapters 1-4 explain its history and theory, while Chapters 5-6 examine the Moral Premise's components and structure.

At the conclusion of each chapter in Part I, there are four suggested exercises. Exercises 1 and 2 ask for a recounting and summary of the material covered in this chapter; these are good for basic reinforcement of the principles. Exercises 3 and 4 ask the reader to extend the learning through expanded reading and writing; these are appropriate for advanced study.

Part II approaches the Moral Premise practically. Chapter 7 suggests some strategic guidelines, Chapter 14 delivers some just-in-time theory on Arc Plots, and Chapter 17 provides a capstone example using *Braveheart*. In between are eight very short chapters, Chapters 8-13 and 15-16, which provide a step-by-step method for embedding a true Moral Premise into a screenplay structured around three acts. Because these chapters lead the reader through a practical application of the theory, there are no additional exercises.

The linear method described in Part II may not suit you. But thinking through the process will broaden your understanding of why and how your intuitive processes work, and how your writing can proceed more efficiently. Given a little bit of faith and discipline the process in Part II can save months of rewrites. After all, the core concept of the Moral Premise and how it works has stood the test of time. It's been around for thousands of years, since stories were first told, and as you'll soon discover, it's proven to be one of the most fundamental structural aspects of storytelling.

It is my hope that *The Moral Premise* will inspire great storytelling... and in the process entertain, delight, challenge, and uplift the generations that come to watch our films.

INTRODUCTION

Today there are many different kinds of movie genres. A rough alphabetical list might include: action, adventure, art, buddy, capers, comedy, coming-of-age, courtroom, crime, detective, disaster, epic, fantasy, film noir, gangster, ghost, historical, horror, love, musicals, myth, road, romance, sci-fi, social, thriller, western, and a dizzying array of hyphenated combinations of all the above. But if any of them are to be successful at the box office there is one thing that must be common to all of them — a true Moral Premise. Regardless of what kind of movie you are going to write or direct, the centrality of the Moral Premise is a story's most important characteristic if you want it to connect with your audience. Let me begin to explain this wonderful phenomenon by simplifying what a movie is about.

All successful movies are about an imperfect protagonist[2] who, in an attempt to improve his life, sets off on a quest toward a physical goal, but along the way is met by a series of physical obstacles of ever-increasing difficulty.

Yeah, you're right. That's old news.

But here's the twist that's as old as storytelling. Every one of those physical obstacles that the protagonist confronts is rooted in a single psychological, spiritual, or emotional obstacle. And to overcome the many physical obstacles, the protagonist must first overcome the singular psychological obstacle that his journey, and the movie, is really about. That single psychological obstacle is summed up by the Moral Premise — *a statement of truth about the protagonist's psychological predicament.*

In successful movies, that psychological truth, or Moral Premise, is offered up to the protagonist in multiple ways and times. But usually

---

2 The term "protagonist" refers to the central dramatic character of a story. The protagonist in a story *does not* always refer to the central "good guy." For instance, in a tragedy, the protagonist is a character that, although we may feel compassion towards him, ultimately fails to achieve his goal. We are more familiar with the protagonist who is a good guy and who succeeds in achieving his or her goal by ultimately overcoming a character flaw. It is this type of protagonist on which this book primarily focuses. I do this only out of convenience and readability, because the rules in this book apply equally to the protagonists of tragedies.

there is one subtly dramatic moment where the Moral Premise is the most clear. Often it's in a scene about half way through the movie. It's an "offering of grace" — a solution to the protagonist's dilemma — that makes crystal clear the fundamental conflict of the protagonist's journey. It's a moment some story theorists call the "Moment of Grace." In that scene, or moment, the protagonist is confronted with an understanding of the human condition in light of the Moral Premise and his own predicament. Although he may not consciously or fully understand the truth that the Moral Premise offers, he still is given a choice to accept the truth or reject it. If the protagonist embraces the truth and tries to apply it to his predicament, the story ends happily. If the protagonist rejects the truth of the Moral Premise, the story ends sadly.

That is a natural law of storytelling structure. If you get it right, your stories or movies have a chance at success. If you get it wrong, regardless of your craft, the budget, star attachments, or marketing efforts, your movie will not be as successful as it could be, if it's successful at all.

This idea of the Moral Premise is not new, but, in fact, is at the heart of all successful storytelling from ancient history right up to the modern day. We find its controlling nature in the writings of Plato, the Bible, and Aesop. We find it in English classics and even the stories we watch on stage and screen.

While the physical and explicit story or plot line is what a movie is about, the psychological and implicit story or plot is what the movie is *really* about. For instance, on the physical, explicit level *Die Hard* is about a New York cop who alone battles an office tower full of desperate, *selfish* thieves. But on the psychological or Moral Premise level the movie is *really* about the depth of one man's *selfless* love for his wife. The motivation of every character in *Die Hard* centers on the conflict and arc between selfishness and selflessness, especially John McClane as he begins the movie selfish, and ends the movie selfless.

Movies are really, at their core, about such psychological and moral things. It is the Moral Premise that affects the structure of the movie as a whole, as well as each act, sequence, scene, and every line of dialogue. It is the Moral Premise that helps the screenwriter, in the first place, to answer the myriad questions that need to be answered about character, setting, conflict, et cetera, and the subsequent decisions made by the producer, film director, casting director, actors, director of photography, production designer, and composer.

Many successful filmmakers make decisions about their stories instinctively. Many do not think consciously about the Moral Premise or how it controls the creative decision-making process. But undergirding their decisions, the Moral Premise has guided their vision. To the extent that their take on the psychological theme or Moral Premise is correct, they will connect with the audience on a spectacular and visceral level.

Now let's get going. Before we get to the how-to part, we really should understand the communication problems and opportunities that confront us.

I

History & Theory

PART

The chapters in this part
examine the Moral Premise's
definition, its use in history
and modern time, relate it to
natural law, define its
structure, and demonstrate how
the Moral Premise is used
to help the filmmaker connect
with the audience through
character identification.

PREMISES AND VALUES

USES OF "PREMISE"

There are a number of different ways in which the term "premise" is used in our culture. They all flow from the same root, yet, depending on industry and context, the meanings are different. It's important that we understand the difference so the rest of this book is clear.

One use of *premise* refers to the *statement(s) of evidence in a logical argument*. Philosophy professor T. Edward Damer, in his book *Attacking Faulty Reasoning*, uses the term *premise* to help define an argument:

> An argument, then, is a group of statements [the *premises*], one or more of which support or provide evidence for another [the *conclusion*].[3]

R. W. Burch, a logician, also refers to premises in a similar way in *A Concise Introduction to Logic*:

> An argument is a group of statements, the purpose of which is that some of them [the *premises*] should support, imply, provide evidence for, or make reasonable to believe another particular one of them [the *conclusion*].[4]

In other words, formal logic uses the term "premise" to simply mean a statement of evidence or a statement of conclusion. In a court of law, the evidences presented to the jury are *evidence premises*, and the conclusion that the attorneys want the jury to arrive at is called a *concluding premise*.

As the insightful reader will discover, each scene of a well-structured and successful movie provides (to the audience/jury) some level of psychological *evidence* toward the movie's psychological *conclusion*, and the more consistently and truthfully that *evidence* is presented, the more believable will be the film's *conclusion*. But we're jumping ahead. Let's get back to defining just the term *premise*.

---

[3] Damer, p 4.
[4] Burch, p. 1.

The second use of *premise* returns us to the entertainment industry and is the *explicit* or denotative story line of a film or television program, like a log line. For example, the explicit premise of *Fly Away Home* can be stated as: "A 13-year-old loses her mother and then takes on the care and raising of a nest full of orphaned goslings."[5] Another example is this explicit premise statement for *City Slickers*: "Three men attempt to deal with their mid-life crises by going on exotic adventures; this time, they go on a cattle round-up and learn a few things about cowboys and themselves."[6] In this book, I'll refer to this use of premise as simply the movie's log line or storyline.

Underneath the storyline, and supported by each scene's evidence, is the third use of the term *premise* — the dramatic heart of a story or film — what I call the *Moral Premise*. In Aristotle's *Poetics*, translator J. Hutton refers to the Moral Premise when he writes about the importance of "The poet's steady aim... the plot... must be the imitation of a unified action comprising a whole."[7] Michael Hauge, in *Writing Screenplays that Sell*, refers to the Moral Premise as the film's *theme*, which for *Tootsie* Hauge writes is: "For relationships to succeed, they must be based on honesty and friendship."[8] Hauge also calls the film's theme the "underlying level of morality... explored through the film" and the "universal statement the movie makes about the human condition."[9]

To understand the critical nature of the Moral Premise in films, however, we need to go deeper. To help us do that we look closely at how Lajos Egri defines *premise*.

LAJOS EGRI'S *PREMISE*

In 1946 Lajos Egri wrote *The Art of Dramatic Writing*, a book I've seen on more than one Hollywood writer's bookshelf. It is still in print. Other authors rarely reference Egri these days, in part I suppose because all of the prolific examples in his book are not movies but stage plays (some obscure and some classic). Yet Egri explains what we should all know as writers, and which the book you're holding attempts to update.

5 *Showtime* Internet movie listings. *http://www.mtv.com/movies/movie/111450/plot.jhtml*
6 *Curran, S. et al*, no page number.
7 Hutton, pp. 64, 54.
8 Hauge, p. 82.
9 Hauge, p. 74.

Egri calls the controlling idea or theme of a story simply the *premise*, and for 296 pages defines its central importance. Egri expounds on why it is the [moral] premise that defines the singular dramatic arc of the story and every character in it. With detailed examples and practical insight, Egri describes how the outward action of a character has no undergirding motivation without the [moral] premise. *Thought always precedes action*, he reminds us, and describes how the kindly Aunt Clara may make a fascinating character study because she takes "such devilish joy in making a lot of trouble for innocent people."[10] But as a writer you don't have a dramatic story until you understand [psychologically] why Aunt Clara interferes so maliciously. It is that "why" that helps to articulate the Moral Premise, and around which every other decision for the story hinges. It is Aunt Clara's inner motivation that reveals the secrets of her character so that you can understand her outward action and set her on the journey toward her goal.

Egri's dramatic heart of a story, what I call the *Moral Premise*, is what the story is all about at the implicit level, or what a logician might define as the *conclusion* of the film's argument. Egri points to *Romeo and Juliet's* premise: "Great love defies even death;" and to *Macbeth's* premise: "Ruthless ambition leads to its own destruction."[11] Note that these premises are moral in nature, they naturally make judgments of what is right and wrong, that is, love is right, ruthless ambition is wrong.

More importantly, Egri enlarges the concept of *premise* by telling of a man running down the street who is intercepted and asked where he is going. "How should I know where I'm going? I am on my way," he answers.[12] This, of course, is an absurd answer, as anyone sprinting with such determination must have a goal, a destination, or conclusion to his journey. Egri's premise then is the *goal*, the destination, or the story's conclusion. And such a destination must not only be clear for the screenwriter, but also to the screenplay's reader, the director, and the movie's audience. Egri elaborates for the would-be playwright:

---

[10] Egri, p.9.
[11] Egri, pp.3–8.
[12] Egri, p.1.

Our aim is to point to a road on which anyone who can write may travel and eventually find himself with a sure approach to drama. So, the *very first thing* you must have is a premise. And it must be a premise worded so that anyone can understand it as the author intended it to be understood. An unclear premise is as bad as no premise at all.

The author using a badly worded, false, or badly constructed premise finds himself filling space and time with pointless dialogue — even action — and not getting anywhere near the proof of his premise. Why? Because he has no direction. [italics added] [13]

When Egri speaks of "filling space and time with pointless dialogue — even action," he refers to writing scenes of the play (or film) that do not support, with evidence, the premise, goal, or psychological conclusion of the film. Egri wants to persuade the playwright to create scenes of evidence that support or argue the "proof" of the conclusion or the premise of the play, or movie in our case.

MESSAGE vs. THEME vs. MORAL PREMISE

Let me make clear that in the context of the book you're holding, the terms *message*, *theme*, and *Moral Premise* are similar but not the same. Some people may interpret the term "message" to mean a "political message" such as "Drilling for oil in the ocean risks the destruction of ocean life as we know it." Such a political message has something to say to a particular group, in a limited region, at a point in time. But in the context of this book, the term "message" is not so limited. This book is not talking about political messages, but rather universal messages.

A "theme" is more often understood to be a universal truth that applies to just about all people, throughout all time, and in all places. For example, a theme might be, "For relationships to succeed, they must be based on honesty and friendship," [14] which is Hauge's take on *Tootsie*. Hauge writes, "[The theme] is the filmmaker's way of saying, 'This is how to be a better human being.'" [15] As I discuss later, the theme

[13] Egri, p.7.
[14] Hauge, p.82.
[15] Hauge, p.74.

is actually one half of the full Moral Premise, although implicit in the theme is the entire Moral Premise concept. In the immediate chapters I may use the terms interchangeably, but I will clarify their practical difference in Chapter 5.

For some writers, settling on the Moral Premise is the first decision they make when writing a new script. Novelist, playwright, and screenwriter Jonathan Gems, who has worked on several films including *1984*, *Batman*, and *Mars Attacks!*, gives this advice: "I figure out the theme before I come up with the actual story. Then I construct a story that tells the theme." Egri concurs:

> Every good play must have a well-formulated [moral] premise.... No idea, and no situation, was ever strong enough to carry you through to its logical conclusion *without a clear-cut premise*.
>
> If you have no such premise, you may modify, elaborate, vary your original idea or situation, or even lead yourself into another situation, but you will not know where you are going. You will flounder, rack your brain to invent further situations to round out your play. You may find these situations — and you will still be without a play.
>
> *You must have a premise* — a premise which will lead you unmistakably to the goal your play hopes to reach.[16]

Moral Premises are important because they articulate first to the writer and then to the audience what the movie is *really* about. To the writer, this means there is a short sentence or phrase by which to measure the writing of each scene to ensure its focus. To the audience, the Moral Premise provides a gathering point for the many thoughts and ideas that may have appeared spurious or random up to a particular juncture in the story. Toward the end, these thoughts and ideas point boldly at what the earlier scenes were all about. This gathering, scene by scene, indicates the writer's moral position about the underlying topic.

In drama, driving the action forward toward a common purpose is all-important. To keep each scene focused on the premise, or, in other words, to ensure that each scene is providing evidence in support of the

---

[16] Egri, p.6.

argument's conclusion, Egri suggests that "a good premise is a thumbnail synopsis of your play."[17] Thus, Egri's premise "Frugality leads to waste" can be a synopsis for a story in which a frugal character refuses to pay his taxes (frugality) and is subsequently caught (leads to) and forced to pay a huge penalty (waste). Each and every scene must reinforce some aspect of this three-part conclusion or the argument of the film is weakened, lessening the audience's conviction that the premise is true or right. Egri writes:

> There are many solutions for any given situation, [but] *your characters are permitted to choose only those which will help prove the premise*. The moment you decide upon a premise, you and your characters become its slave. Each character must feel, intensely, that the action dictated by the premise is the *only action possible*. [italics in original] [18]

This consistency of the Moral Premise to which Egri alludes — in each action and each scene — is the keystone of a story's success. Just as the Moral Premise describes the conflict that should appear in each scene, so each scene reinforces the conflict summarized by the Moral Premise.

Now, this is a good place to shift our discussion to what precipitates a story's moral conflict, securing your understanding of *why* the Moral Premise is so important.

CONFLICT OF VALUES

Joel Silvers, a university screenwriting and filmmaking instructor, suspects that before students can understand story structure, they must first understand that the physical or outward conflict grows out of an inner conflict of values. Only after there is a clear understanding of the inner conflict of values can a characters make a value-oriented decision that has the potential of physical action. With such a value conflict in the psychological air, the structure of physical conflict makes a lot more sense to talk about.[19] For in a movie, as opposed to a novel, the principal conflict must be physical and visible. But even in a novel, action is inevitable, and that action is always based on a set of values that are in conflict between characters.

---

[17] Egri, p.8.
[18] Egri, p.1151.
[19] Joel Silvers, personal communication, March 25, 2005.

This awareness of the importance of conflict between values is critical to formulating a Moral Premise, which articulates the psychological spine of good stories. Psychologically, a set of values is the fertilizer for ideas, ideologies, and thoughts that course through our mind and soul and gives us motivation to take action. If filmmakers, therefore, do not understand the basic need of stories to grow from the conflict of values, then the filmmaker's attempts at filmmaking will be nothing more than the unmotivated juxtapositions of images and sound. It is the lack of a story based in the conflict of values structured around a Moral Premise that leaves audiences with a sense that the movie they just gave two hours of their life to was a wasteland of meaning. Conflict is essential but it must be rooted in values and structured around a Moral Premise.

IDENTIFYING VALUES

It is not unusual to meet young film students, or even adult film enthusiasts, who do not have a clear idea of what a value is. We all have them, but few of us ever stop to think about what they are, or which ones motivate our lives. This is especially disastrous for filmmakers who need to create characters with motivations. So what follows, from three different lists, is an attempt to make us aware of what values are and how they drive the decisions our characters need to make.

Benjamin Franklin's Virtues

The first list will be familiar to those who have read Benjamin Franklin's autobiography. Franklin's thinking related to values directly affects our formulation of Moral Premises. So, here is Franklin's introduction to his list of values, or virtues as he calls them.

> It was about this time I conceiv'd the bold and arduous project of arriving at moral perfection. I wish'd to live without committing any fault at any time; I would conquer all that either natural inclination, custom, or company might lead me into. As I knew, or thought I knew, what was right and wrong, I did not see why I might not always do the one and avoid the other. But I soon found I had undertaken a task of

more difficulty than I had imagined. While my care was employ'd in guarding against one fault, I was often surprised by another; habit took the advantage of inattention; inclination was sometimes too strong for reason. I concluded, at length, that the mere speculative conviction that it was our interest to be completely virtuous, was not sufficient to prevent our slipping; and that the contrary habits must be broken, and good ones acquired and established, before we can have any dependence on a steady, uniform rectitude of conduct. For this purpose I therefore contrived the following method.

Franklin did some research and came up with a list of virtues that he decided were meaningful to his particular proclivity and need for personal improvement. Notice, he recognized that his outward actions were directed by his inner values. Here is his list of virtues, with their precepts as he explained and spelt them.

Table 1 — Benjamin Franklin's Virtues and Precepts	
Temperance	Eat not to dullness; drink not to elevation.
Silence	Speak not but what may benefit others or yourself; avoid trifling conversation.
Order	Let all your things have their places; let each part of your business have its time.
Resolution	Resolve to perform what you ought; perform without fail what you resolve.
Frugality	Make no expense but to do good to others or yourself; i.e., waste nothing.
Industry	Lose no time; be always employ'd in something useful; cut off all unnecessary actions.
Sincerity	Use no hurtful deceit; think innocently and justly, and, if you speak, speak accordingly.
Justice	Wrong none by doing injuries, or omitting the benefits that are your duty.

Moderation	Avoid extremes; forbear resenting injuries so much as you think they deserve.
Cleaniness	Tolerate no uncleanliness in body, clothes, or habitation.
Tranquillity	Be not disturbed at trifles, or at accidents common or unavoidable.
Chastity	Rarely use venery but for health or offspring, never to dullness, weakness, or the injury of your own or another's peace or reputation.
Humility	Imitate Jesus and Socrates.

Intent on turning these values into visible actions Franklin writes:

> I made a little book, in which I allotted a page for each of the virtues. I rul'd each page with red ink, so as to have seven columns, one for each day of the week, marking each column with a letter for the day. I cross'd these columns with thirteen red lines, marking the beginning of each line with the first letter of one of the virtues, on which line, and in its proper column, I might mark, by a little black spot, every fault I found upon examination to have been committed respecting that virtue upon that day.

> I determined to give a week's strict attention to each of the virtues successively. Thus, in the first week, my great guard was to avoid even the least offence against Temperance, leaving the other virtues to their ordinary chance, only marking every evening the faults of the day. Thus, if in the first week I could keep my first line, marked T, clear of spots, I suppos'd the habit of that virtue so much strengthen'd and its opposite weaken'd, that I might venture extending my attention to include the next, and for the following week keep both lines clear of spots. Proceeding thus to the last, I could go thro' a course compleat in thirteen weeks, and four courses in a year.[20]

---

[20] Franklin, pp. 128 ff.

Now the insightful dramatist will, upon surveying such a list as Franklin's, recognize the deep potential such a list provides for dramatic stories. For implicitly juxtaposed next to each of Franklin's virtues is an obvious vice, or potential conflict of values. We can imagine a character, like Franklin, who let's say is a U.S. Ambassador in Paris, where he is invited to dine with French diplomats and offered a glass of rare and expensive French wine. But because our character values temperance to the point of abstinence, the U.S. Ambassador offends his host by refusing to partake of something his French peers would consider a great value. As the night progresses, this initial and subtle conflict over wine escalates into disagreements on other levels that lead to physical, even international conflict.

Hyrum W. Smith's Governing Values

In his book, *The 10 Natural Laws of Successful Time and Life Management*, Hyrum Smith presents a list of "governing values" that resulted from a 1992 nationwide survey conducted by his Franklin Quest Co. To those of you who have ever taken a Franklin Planner seminar or read any number of their books on time management, this list of values will seem familiar. These are ranked in order of frequency of occurrence in the survey results.

Table 2 — Franklin Quest's Survey of Governing Values[21]

1. Spouse	16. Intelligence and wisdom
2. Financial security	17. Understanding
3. Personal health and fitness	18. Quality of life
4. Children and family	19. Happiness/Positive attitude
5. Spirituality/Religion	20. Pleasure
6. A sense of accomplishment	21. Self-control
7. Integrity and honesty	22. Ambition
8. Occupational satisfaction	23. Being capable
9. Love for others/Service	24. Imagination and creativity
10. Education and learning	25. Forgiveness
11. Self-respect	26. Generosity
12. Taking responsibility	27. Equality
13. Exercising leadership	28. Friendship
14. Inner harmony	29. Beauty
15. Independence	30. Courage

[21] Smith, p. 63-64.

Again, the opportunities for conflict and drama from this list are great. First, there is the obvious conflict between any one of these values and its imagined opposite:

Self-respect vs. Self-destruction
Independence vs. Dependence
Equality vs. Bigotry
Forgiveness vs. Bitterness
Courage vs. Cowardice

But, second, there is another level of conflict that provides a more interesting dramatic dilemma — when a virtue is taken so far that it becomes a vice. Integrity and honesty can be taken so far that telling the truth can endanger the lives of those we love. Courage can be misinterpreted or taken so far as to take foolish risks for no noble purpose. Self-respect can turn into arrogance. Defense of freedom can lead to wars that decimate civilizations. Forgiveness can disregard justice that also needs to be served.

In these ways values are the taproot of stories that give our movies meaning and our audiences understanding and satisfaction.

Laurie Beth Jones

Finally, here is a succinct list of values from Laurie Beth Jones' *The Path: The Field Guide*, where she lays out a plan for creating a personal mission statement. One of the steps Jones takes the reader through is the identification of core values that *motivate* one to *action*. I'm pretty sure she wasn't thinking of writing screenplays or creating stories when she came up with this list, but she was thinking of motivating people. Our task as screenwriters and filmmakers, of course, is to motivate characters into and out of dramatic conflict. One of the questions Jones asks her reader is "What concept or principle would you be willing to die for?" That's a great question to ask your protagonist when you're developing his or her character; and an even more important question to ask your antagonist, although the antagonist's willing-to-die-for-value may be the opposite of one in Jones' list.

Table 3 — Laurie Beth Jones' Core Values		
Truth	Self-Worth	Safety
Integrity	Dignity	Relationships
Honesty	Respect	Kindness
Freedom	Inner Peace	Service
Trust	Love	Equality
Faith	Positive Attitude	Excellence
Justice	Hope	Nobility
Wholeness	Joy	Humility
Honor	Charity	Simplicity

Antagonists

Speaking of antagonists, let me clear up a misconception. A story's antagonist is the character or force that opposes the protagonist. We normally think of the antagonist as someone who wants to stop the protagonist at all costs, such as Hans Gruber in *Die Hard*. But the antagonist may be someone who actually wants to help the protagonist, although their outward actions create major obstacles, such as Sergeant Foley in *An Officer and a Gentleman*. The antagonist may also be an unwitting obstacle such as the public's willingness to sue superheroes in *The Incredibles*. Antagonists may also be lovers or friends in romantic comedies such as what Sally is to Harry and Harry is to Sally in *When Harry Met Sally*. In the television series, *Touched by An Angel*, the angels are the antagonists as they throw obstacles in the weekly protagonist's path to help them change. And finally, the story's antagonist may be one's own self such as Bruce Nolan's immaturity in *Bruce Almighty*.

PREMISE GENRES AND CONFLICT OF VALUES

At the beginning of this book I listed a number of film genres. Here is the list a second time, for your convenience.

Table 4 — Movie Genres		
Action	Detective	Love
Adventure	Disaster	Musicals
Art	Epic	Myth
Buddy	Fantasy	Road
Capers	Film Noir	Romance
Comedy	Gangster	Sci-Fi
Coming-of-Age	Ghost	Social
Courtroom	Historical	Thrillers
Crime	Horror	Westerns

While it is outside the scope of this book, each of these genres typically explores a limited number of moral values in conflict. For instance, adventure films frequently explore the conflict of secrecy vs. discovery. Coming-of-age films frequently explore the values of self-expression vs. conformity. Historical dramas are often about the clash of tradition vs. revolution. Science Fiction often sets up a conflict between technology and humanity.

One way to categorize the conflict of values in narratives is to look for them in one of six basic plots expanded from the four in Aristotle's *Poetics*: (1) man against man; (2) man against nature; (3) man against himself; (4) man against the supernatural; (5) man against society; and (6) man against machine.[22]

A more extensive categorization of conflict can be found in Georges Polti's classic work, *The 36 Dramatic Situations* (see Table 5). Polti painstakingly demonstrates that all stories are simply variations of only 36 basic plots that originate from "fundamental human emotional [value] conflicts."

---

22 Aristotle's *Poetics*, XVIII. Baehr's expanded list (p. 176) based on Ingram Bywater's translation identifies the four as: complex, suffering, character, and spectacle. S. H. Butcher's translation lists: complex, pathetic, ethical, and simple. I come up with: (1) reversal of fortune that comes from a surprising discovery; (2) physical suffering that results from misapplied passion; (3) psychological struggle resulting from an ethical dilemma; (4) battle with supernatural forces.

Table 5 — George Polti's 36 Dramatic Situations[23]

1. Supplication	20. Self-sacrificing for an ideal
2. Deliverance	21. Self-sacrifice for kindred
3. Crime pursued by vengeance	22. All sacrificed for a passion
4. Vengeance taken for kindred upon kindred	23. Necessity of sacrificing loved ones
5. Pursuit	24. Rivalry of superior and inferior
6. Disaster	25. Adultery
7. Falling prey to cruelty or misfortune	26. Crimes of love
8. Revolt	27. Discovery of the dishonor of a loved one
9. Daring enterprise	28. Obstacles to love
10. Abduction	29. An enemy loved
11. The enigma	30. Ambition
12. Obtaining	31. Conflict with a god
13. Enmity of kinsmen	32. Mistaken jealousy
14. Rivalry of kinsmen	33. Erroneous judgment
15. Murderous adultery	34. Remorse
16. Madness	35. Recovery of a lost one
17. Fatal imprudence	36. Loss of loved ones
18. Involuntary crimes of love	
19. Slaying of a kinsman unrecognized	

Conflict in these classifications describes not only the physical drama of the explicit premise but also the psychological drama of the Moral Premise.

❧

There are, however, some modern critics (and paid story consultants) who claim that for films to be popular they do not need a moral center or a Moral Premise. Research[24] suggests, however, that when other production values, attachments, and distribution are in place, the film with a strong moral center will succeed; but when a moral center is

---

23 Polti, p. 3.
24 See the Appendix.

missing or inconsistently applied, regardless of the other production values, attachments, or distribution, the ticket sales will always disappoint. Even putting research aside, a cursory examination will affirm that psychological moral dilemmas are at the heart of every successful story. Cynical storytellers and consultants may want to deny that fact, but they will never abandon it in their own stories. And in the next chapter we'll take a look at a number of examples of the moral essence of storytelling throughout history.

In the Bedroom's Moment of Grace — Father McClasslin sits with Ruth Fowler at her son's gravesite, offering her the opportunity to ask forgiveness for the anger she confesses — the literal offering of grace through the Sacrament of Reconciliation (Confession). © 2001, Miramax Films

EXERCISES

1. List and define the different uses of the term "premise."

2. Contrast and compare the terms "message," "theme," and "Moral Premise" as they apply to stories and especially motion picture narratives.

3. Moral Premises are rooted in values. Select a number of film genres from the list in this chapter, and for each, list two conflicting values that a film in the genre might explore. Explain how those values are germane to the genre.

4. To expand your awareness of basic dramatic conflict, choose a number of Polti's dramatic situations and for each: (1) identify two characters with opposing values; and (2) describe how the contrasting values of these characters might create a dramatic situation worthy of a story.

WHAT SOCRATES AND
SEINFELD HAVE IN COMMON

2

A Moral Premise describes a story's moral meaning. The moral meaning of story messages is the cornerstone of historical and popular narrative and is the reason stories, in general, are so important to us as human beings. This chapter briefly examines narrative history and the use of moral themes in fiction. We will first define the concept of what is *moral*, and second how Moral Premises have been discussed and used in narrative forms from antiquity to the present day.

WEBSTER

The term *moral* has many connotations and is often misunderstood. My Webster describes ten usages of the term. Here are the first and last of them:

> **mor•al** *adj.* **1.** of, pertaining to, or concerned with the principles of right conduct or the distinction between right and wrong; ethical: *moral attitudes.* **2.** conforming to accepted or established principles of right conduct (opposed to *immoral*); virtuous; upright: a *moral man....* —n. **9.** the moral teaching or practical lesson contained in a fable, tale, experience, etc. **10. morals**, principles, standards, or habits with respect to right or wrong conduct.[25]

It is interesting that the first eight most common usages of "moral" are adjectives, which is the principle way I'm using the term in this book (*Moral Premise*), and that the most common usage as a noun (albeit in 9th place) pertains to the same thing. A Moral Premise *is the practical lesson of a story*. What I really want to point out, however, is that the term *moral* does not literally refer to just what is right, but rather to the discourse of the distinction between what is right and

---

[25] Costello.

wrong. That means any juxtaposition between what is perceived as right and what is perceived as wrong is moral in nature. And that most such juxtapositions lead us naturally to *conflict* — the element without which storytelling cannot exist.

Later, I refer to the *evidence* of an argument as being either valid or invalid, and, as used in this book, *valid* does correspond to both a logical and a general social perception of *rightness*, or put another way, the evidence is *without fallacy*. Conversely, *invalid* corresponds to both an illogical and a general social perception of *wrongness*, or put another way, the evidence is *fallacious*, or *with fallacy*. For the extent of the present book, however, a *moral* issue is neither *valid* nor *invalid*, but rather an issue the writer deals with as simply having a *right* and *wrong* side. Speaking of right and wrong, what better place to bring up a best seller on the topic.

THE BIBLE

Considering stories about right and wrong, the oldest long-form story is that of the Jewish nation as told in what is commonly known as the Old Testament — the epitome of moral tales complete with ten very well-known, although not very well observed, moral messages — *The Ten Commandments*.

Table 6 - The Original Moral Messages: The Ten Commandments[26]

   I. You shall have no other gods before me.
   II. You shall not misuse the name of the LORD your God...
   III. Remember the Sabbath day by keeping it holy...
   IV. Honor your father and your mother...
   V. You shall not murder.
   VI. You shall not commit adultery.
   VII. You shall not steal.
   VIII. You shall not give false testimony against your neighbor.
   IX. You shall not covet your neighbor's wife.
   X. You shall not covet your neighbor's possessions.

[26] Jewish, Protestant, and Catholic texts all number the commandments differently even though they're all from the same text, Exodus 20:3-17. The listing here is the Catholic version.

A log line for the Old Testament could be: The story of the Tribes of Israel and how God led their ancestors from Ur (Iraq) to Egypt, and finally to Palestine, only to then be dispersed into near oblivion. When the Israelites obeyed the Ten Commandments they fared pretty well. When the Israelites disobeyed the Ten Commandments they found themselves at the wrong end of a sword or a lightning bolt.

Each Commandment can be seen as an abbreviated moral theme leading to a Moral Premise. Take the story about the Golden Calf. While the explicit or physical premise of that story is about the Israelites melting down their Egyptian jewelry to make an idol, the psychological or Moral Premise of the story is about the Israelites' rejection of Yahweh's First Commandment (you shall have no other gods before me) and the resulting consequences. The Israelites' psychological thoughts dictated their physical actions. *Their actions were the result of their thoughts.* On the surface, the story seems to be about making a Golden Calf, but psychologically it's really about making moral choices to worship a God other than Yahweh. And, as we'll see, good stories are about that very thing — the making of a moral (psychological) choice that results in a physical action, and ends in a physical and psychological consequence.

Although mentioning the Ten Commandments may bring to mind Cecil B. DeMille's 1956 pageantry and spectacle, a more apt example of the use of the Ten Commandments as the basis for a film's Moral Premise comes from Krzysztof Kieslowski's award-winning *The Decalogue*. Here, in ten one-hour films, Kieslowski uses the Ten Commandments as a springboard for exploring everyday moral dilemmas that haunt the inhabitants of an apartment complex in Poland during communist rule. Kieslowski said his films are "an attempt to return to elementary values destroyed by communism."[27]

The New Testament also contains many well-known stories whose primary purpose was the communication of moral themes such as this collection from Christ's Sermon on the Mount:

> Blessed are the poor in spirit, for theirs is the kingdom
> of heaven.

---

[27] Quoted in Hibbs, Thomas (2003). *Kieslowski's Fundamentals: Values in ten acts.* http://www.nationalreview.com/comment/hibbs200312230101.asp

Blessed are they who mourn, for they will be comforted.

Blessed are the meek, for they will inherit the land.

Blessed are they who hunger and thirst for righteousness, for they will be satisfied.

Blessed are the merciful, for they will be shown mercy.

Blessed are the clean of heart, for they will see God.

Blessed are the peacemakers, for they will be called children of God.

Blessed are they who are persecuted for the sake of righteousness, for theirs is the kingdom of heaven.

Blessed are you when they insult you and persecute you and utter every kind of evil against you (falsely) because of me.[28]

These too, like the Ten Commandments, are the psychological, or spiritual themes that become the moral basis for the many stories that appear in the New Testament, both in the form of parables and in the historical accounts of the early Christian Church.

While we might expect moral lessons to be explicit in Bible stories, for the most part they are implicit and the lessons indirect. Rev. Jesse Hurlbut, an author of Bible lesson materials and storybooks during the first half of the 20th century, explains this in his introduction to his then-popular *Story of the Bible*. What I find interesting about this description is that it applies to modern motion pictures as well.

Stories have deeper meanings and a spiritual significance that the child does not comprehend. These come home to the adult, and with added force if he realizes that these are the stories that he heard at his mother's knee. While if read for the first time, they are beautiful as literature, interesting as stories, and of the greatest value in touching the heart and awakening the conscience.[29]

Hurlbut realized what successful filmmakers do today (especially those who craft popular animated features) — that explicit or physical story lines can be targeted to children, yet all ages, including adults, can grasp the importance and significance of the story's psychological or moral message that ignites our conscience.

---

[28] Matthew 5:3-11. New American Bible.
http://www.nccbuscc.org/nab/bible/matthew/matthew3.htm
[29] Hurlbut, p. 9.

AESOP

The collection of *Aesop's Fables* (circa 650 B.C.) is an obvious example of moral storytelling. The fables, in various forms, are still in "print" such as Project Gutenberg's E-text (1995), which documents 306 fables. Many of these fables contain explicit Moral Premises such as "Evil wishes, like chickens, come home to roost" (No. 32. The Bee and Jupiter); and "The safeguards of virtue are hateful to those with evil intentions" (No. 264. The Thieves and the Cock). George Fyler Townsend (1814-1900), the translator of the fables used by Project Gutenberg, writes about the moral message built into these ancient fantasies, and relates them to vice and virtue, two critical elements of a true Moral Premise.

> [The fable] will ever keep in view, as its high prerogative, and inseparable attribute, the great purpose of instruction, and will necessarily seek to inculcate some moral maxim, social duty, or political truth... the true fabulist [story teller], therefore, discharges a most important function. He is neither a narrator, nor an allegorist. He is a great teacher, a corrector of morals, a censor of vice, and a commender of virtue.[30]

Aesop, the Phrygian, was perhaps the earliest documented expert on the existence of Moral Premises in stories. Born a slave, he earned his liberty as a reward for his learning and wit, and raised himself to high renown. Finding a place in public service as the monarch's emissary, he traveled to small republics of Greece and helped reconcile the inhabitants and settle public affairs by telling these stories.[31]

Aesop's ability to connect with his audience and convince them of the wise and right thing to do through the use of his stories is the same thing that happens today when audiences learn from movies the wise and right thing to do.

One of the reasons Aesop's stories were, and why movies are, so powerful has to do with the power of metaphors. Aesop and successful filmmakers are good at making metaphors. French philosopher Paul Ricoeur in *Time and Narrative* explains that the combination of

---

[30] Translator's notes in Aesop, no page number.

[31] An abbreviated story of Aesop's life can be found on the Gutenberg website.

"time" and "narrative" creates a metaphor that brings new meaning through the combination of discrete visuals and otherwise dry discourse. Separate and unrelated ideas are craftily put together into a story, and a new meaning takes shape in what Ricoeur calls a "semantic innovation." The new meaning is the result of the productive imagination of the storyteller who has become skilled at "inaugurating" the similarness of things that "at first seem 'distant,' then suddenly 'close.'"[32] That closeness, which rises suddenly in the eyes and hearts of the audience, is the dawn of a new understanding or meaning of things that comes out of the juxtaposition and combination of narrative elements — plot, character, setting, conflict, and Moral Premise. Audiences come to stories looking for answers or hints about life's meaning. And when stories give them new insights they're given fresh hope for a better future. That is what made the ancient Aesop's Fables legendary and why modern films are so popular.

But there was more to Aesop's popularity (and good stories in general) than just creating new meaning through a story's juxtapositions and combinations. In his essay on *The Catholic Imagination*, novelist, social researcher, and priest Andrew Greeley hints at the attraction of good stories by suggesting that it is through stories (principally from the past) that religions and societies arrive at doctrines and social rules of order. In Catholicism, he writes, ancient stories are told with moral significance, and their lessons kept alive, through:

> an enchanted world... of statues and holy water, stained glass and votive candles, saints and religious medals, rosary beads and holy pictures.... Churches are treasure houses of stories [which] are as important now as they ever were. Religion is *story* before it is anything else and after it is everything else.[33]

Greeley reminds us that it was the stories of the churches that motivated the artists and benefactors to create the art for which the church, in its past at least, was famous. It was through the abundance of morally significant storytelling in the church that:

> the miracle and morality plays sprang out of the liturgical

---

[32] Ricoeur, p. x.
[33] Greeley, p. 35.

cycle at the altar, gathered force as performance inside the church during non-liturgical hours, and finally broke forth into the cathedral plaza as plays for the general populace. Similarly, the oratorios developed out of the polyphonic masses, gradually moved into the theaters, and eventually became operas [and movies].[34]

The stories that emanated from churches, of course, had the same purpose as Aesop's Fables — they were designed to tell us something about the human condition and how it can be improved by the moral decisions we make. There is something very natural and fundamental about stories that capture our attention and imagination. Stories tell us what we long to know — why we're here and how we can make the best of it. Stories fundamentally and naturally satisfy man's search for the meaning of life.

SOCRATES

During the time of Plato, the Greek state had ordered poets to express only the image of the good in their work, or suffer physical pain. Their concern was not just a philosophical search of life's meaning, but also a proper moral education for their youth. At the beginning of Book III of Plato's *Republic*, Socrates, in dialogue with friends, describes the significance of aural and visual arts in the moral education of youth and explains why arts of "moral deformity" should be withheld from society:

> Is the same control to be extended to other artists [musicians, gymnasts and dramatists]... are they also to be prohibited from exhibiting the opposite forms of vice and intemperance and meanness and indecency in sculpture and building and the other creative arts...? We would not have our guardians [read: children] grow up amid images of moral deformity, as in some noxious pasture, and there browse and feed upon many a baneful herb and flower day by day, little by little, until they silently gather a festering

---

[34] Greeley, pp. 34-35.

mass of corruption in their own soul. Let our artists rather be those who are gifted to discern the true nature of the beautiful and graceful; then will our youth dwell in a land of health, amid fair sights and sounds, and receive the good in everything.[35]

In this manner Socrates, through Plato (and also Aristotle as we'll see in the next chapter),[36] positioned art and drama as instruments of moral instruction.

ENGLISH CLASSICS

The long-form narrative works of the 17th and 18th centuries were written to communicate other moral messages. From the quill of Ben Jonson in 1610 came *The Alchemist* in which editor McCollum states that Jonson "flays pretense, affectation, hypocrisy, greed, and lust."[37] John Milton's *Paradise Lost*, penned in 1667, is about how "true freedom lies in obedience and obedience is not bondage."[38] In 1678, John Bunyan published *Pilgrim's Progress*, a masterful allegory about how the downtrodden, the poor, and the humble have God as their moral guide.[39] Lesser known as a moral tome, perhaps, is Henry Fielding's 1742 novel *The History of the Adventures of Joseph Andrews*,[40] and better known, in 1749, *The History of Tom Jones*.[41] These two novels are noteworthy, not because they lampoon the morals of the era in which they were written, but because they are explicit in stating that there is a

---

[35] Plato, p. 288.

[36] I sometimes get these three Greek guys mixed up. Here is their relation to each other. In order of their lives: Socrates (469-399 BC) was the stonecutter and great oral philosopher who never wrote anything but went around asking a lot of questions — the Socratic Method. Socrates mentored Plato (427-347 BC) who came up with a lot of the answers and wrote down a great deal including Socrates' discussions in the books of *Republic*. Plato also started an academy of learning at which the younger Aristotle (384-322 BC) was a student. According to these dates, when Socrates drank the State's hemlock at the age of 70, Plato was 28, and Aristotle 15.

[37] Jonson, p. ix.

[38] Shawcross, p. 249.

[39] Bunyan.

[40] Fielding, 2001.

[41] Fielding, 1998.

moral message attached. Consider the first two paragraphs from the opening salvo of Joseph Andrews wherein Fielding writes:

> It is a trite but true observation that examples work more forcibly on the mind than precepts;[42] and if this be just in what is odious and blamable, it is more strongly so in what is amiable and praiseworthy. Here emulation more effectually operates upon us, and inspires our imitation in an irresistible manner. A good man therefore is a standing lesson to all his acquaintance, and of far greater use in that narrow circle than a good book.
>
> But as it often happens that the best men are but little known, and consequently cannot extend the usefulness of their examples a great way; the writer may be called in aid to spread their history farther, and to present the amiable pictures to those who have not the happiness of knowing the originals; and so, by communicating such valuable patterns to the world, they may perhaps do a more extensive service to mankind than the person whose life originally afforded the pattern.[43]

If that all seems a little esoteric, here's a brief translation: *Stories about bad characters confronted by good, are more helpful than stories about good characters trying to be good.* There's drama in the former but not in the latter. And, remember what a movie is about — an imperfect protagonist attempting to improve his life.

In the first of the two quoted paragraphs above, terms like *precepts, odious, blamable, amiable, good,* and *lesson* more than call our attention to the moral slant of the pages that will follow. The second paragraph goes further and praises the novel as the carrier of a valued message, with phrases as "extend the usefulness... a great way," "spread their history farther," and "service to mankind." In this way, Fielding is explicit about his intent to communicate a moral message to society. The point I am trying to make is that it does not matter

[42] Compare Fielding's comment with Andrew Greeley's conclusions in *The Catholic Imagination* that precepts (church doctrine) originate out of stories.

[43] Fielding, 2001, p. 1.

whether the moral message is valid or invalid, but rather that throughout history stories have existed primarily to communicate moral messages.[44]

CRITICISM

Such is the case, as well, with novel criticism of the 18th century, when the story-verisimilitude phenomenon (i.e., the importance that critics put on the story in society's search for truth) concerned itself not only with the moral implications of the story, but the technique of telling it, as exampled in this passage on fiction from Dr. Samuel Johnson in 1750:

> In narratives where historical veracity has no place, I cannot discover why there should not be exhibited the most perfect idea of virtue; of virtue not angelical, nor above probability (for what we cannot credit, we shall never imitate), but the highest and purest that humanity can reach.[45]

Such sentiments can be described only as idealism, a philosophy that narrative theorist J. Halperin traced in novel-theory of the 18th century. Critics at that time concerned themselves not so much with the morality of the tale but with the morality of the novelist's technique. Halperin describes idealism not as the antithesis of realism (which was argued significantly at that time) but idealism as the basis of all art. He concludes that novel-theory, well into the 18th and 19th centuries, saw idealism as truth uncorrupted and realism's antithesis as "falsism."[46] These were concepts from writers and critics who easily detected the moral implications in messages.

---

[44] This is to say nothing of the great many books and articles that lampooned Fielding for the "immoral" tale of *Tom Jones*. Samuel Richardson (author of *Pamela* that Fieldings' *Joseph Andrews* satires) wrote that Fielding is "the inventor of that cant phrase goodness of heart, which is every day used as a substitute for probity, and means little more than the virtue of a horse or a dog: in short, he has done more towards corrupting the rising generation than any writer we know of" (cited in Harrison, p. 10). It is reported that *Pamela* was the first novel printed in the English language. If true, *Joseph Andrews* was the second.
[45] Halperin, p. 4.
[46] Halperin, p. 8.

MODERN STORIES

Whether we look at the novel, television, or film, moral messages are everywhere. For instance, *A Time To Kill*, as a book and as a film, is about how "faithfulness leads to justice for both the innocent and the guilty" or how "unjust hatred leads to a just death." *Clear and Present Danger*, as a book and as a film, is explicitly about a version of the "might is right" theme, except here it is "technological might is right." If, in the spy genre, rightness is protected by secrecy, then the moral message of *Clear and Present Danger* could be "silence is the greatest passion of all."[47] This would be a fit message for a spy thriller as the drug cartel, the U.S. military, and lovers create conflict and solution by their silence while satellites, in perfect silence, create impassioned links for the U.S. to carry out its zeal for information and quest for justice. *The Prince of Tides*, as a book and as a film, reveals how love can heal a violent past and "make something beautiful out of the ruins."[48]

On the television side of the moral issue, the 200+ episodes of *Married with Children* seems to lampoon the very idea that interpersonal or social morality exists. But beneath the surface, the humor finds its resonance in the negative consequence of the Bundy family's rejection of societal moral norms. The Bundys are white trash: indifferent, parasitic losers and moral degenerates who suffer the consequences.[49] But, at the same time, they stick together because they're a family. As Al, the father, has often said: "Bundys are losers, not quitters." Although the explicit treatments were often obnoxious to conservative audiences, the Moral Premise of *Married with Children's* parody is nonetheless a resounding (albeit backdoor) endorsement of conservative moral values.

Seinfeld is about the rightness and wrongness of the small stuff; whether George has gravy or butter on his potatoes has a "rightness" as significant as fornication. Is fornication (or adultery) wrong? For the answer, watch the facial reaction (is there anything else?) of television soap opera stars when they discover that their "significant

[47] Clancy, pp. 124-125, 688. The last phrase in the novel is: "Silence was the greatest passion of all."
[48] Conroy, pp. 649, 657.
[49] The title of the show used in early pitches was reported as "Not the Cosbys" (i.e. *The Huxtables*.

other" has done "it." *Home Improvement* focuses on doing what is right for your family, complete with moral lessons that come from a "mystical," all-knowing neighbor.

Wherever we look, read or listen, there are moral messages. Even politicos who pontificate that their peers across the aisle are *wrong* for pushing their brand of morality, are in fact pushing their own brand of morality. Besides, are not all laws efforts to legislate and define right from wrong? Suggesting what is right and wrong, whether through propositional statements in a religion's catechism, or negotiating and passing a public law, enforcing it, and adjudicating it, or telling stories that have implicit and even subtle Moral Premises, are all normal moral acts of human beings. It's what we do in our search for truth and meaning.

But some "politically correct" aficionados still claim that pushing moral messages is a moral wrong. Bill Maher's *Politically Incorrect* had a good run off of such irony. Although we are surrounded by moral messages (even in advertising, into which I dare not roam), the authors that tell us how to construct and tell our stories and write our screenplays seem to tiptoe around the fact that most messages are essentially, well... ah... moral.

Bruce Nolan's Moment of Grace in *Bruce Almighty*. After a day of expecting miracles on his behalf and getting them in the form of God's power, Bruce wakes up the next morning hearing the prayers of the people around him. Thus begins his journey of discovery that where grace and gifts are given, there is also the responsibility of being the miracle for others. © 2003, Universal Studios

EXERCISES

1. Write a brief essay that describes the similarities of how stories have communicated moral themes through the ages.

2. List a number of modern and popular television episodic programs and describe the moral themes that each explores.

3. Write a brief review of an 18th- or 19th-century classic novel in terms of how it communicates moral values and themes. Identify the themes and the characters that espouse conflicting values that give the story dramatic force.

4. Examine several communication channels not discussed in this chapter, such as cable news, blogs, comic books or games, and describe the moral themes and values each advances.

THE MORAL PREMISE IN
MODERN WRITING GUIDES

3

As important as themes and Moral Premises are to movies, few books on screenwriting give them significant treatment. And when the concept of the Moral Premise is discussed, different authors use different terms and it is dealt with in varying degrees. I think it's time to consolidate the various concepts, definitions, and treatments and assign a singular term. For that term I suggest "The Moral Premise," and this book is my attempt at the consolidation. Allow me, therefore, to take the time to comment on what a number of contemporary authors, in their own terms, say about the "moral premise." Then I will make an effort to pull the theory together under a common banner and suggest practical steps for its use.

ROBERT MCKEE'S *CONTROLLING IDEA*

Robert McKee's *Story* refers to a film's Moral Premise as its *controlling idea*, which he defines as "the story's ultimate meaning expressed through the action and aesthetic emotion of the last act's climax."[50]

McKee also describes how that controlling idea is demonstrated through the spine of the main character's quest, whether that spine be a conscious or unconscious object of desire, or both. The process the protagonist goes through to achieve the quest has two kinds of events: those that thrust the protagonist closer to his goal ("positive charge"), and those that obstruct this forward momentum ("negative charge"). This roller coaster ride toward the goal is described by the *controlling idea*.

> A CONTROLLING IDEA may be expressed in a single sen-
> tence describing how and why life undergoes change from
> one condition of existence at the beginning to another at the
> end.... [it's] the purest form of a story's meaning, the how
> and why of change, the vision of life the audience members
> carry away into their lives.[51]

---

[50] McKee, p 115.
[51] McKee, p 115, 117.

McKee's controlling idea is a good bridge to the point I need to make about the Moral Premise. The way he expresses the concept is slightly different and narrower in focus than my Moral Premise. But he understands that there is an idea, a concept, a single thought that summarizes and possibly even controls the story and all the subplots in that story — a point I make explicit later on. In other words, the controlling idea for McKee describes the "arc" of the story. And he gives the following examples:

> *Dirty Harry*: Justice triumphs because the protagonist is more violent than the criminals.
> *Columbo* (TV series): Justice is restored because the protagonist is cleverer than the criminal.
> *Groundhog Day*: Happiness fills our lives when we learn to love unconditionally.

What I'll suggest and demonstrate later is that the Moral Premise is not so different from McKee's controlling idea, except that the Moral Premise applies not just to the protagonist and the main storyline but also to all the principal characters and subplots as well.

For the time being, however, let's examine a few other books, for there is much to learn from such analysis, as we add to and consolidate their combined wisdom.

MICHAEL TIERNO'S *THE ACTION-IDEA*

In Aristotle's *Poetics for Screenwriters*, Michael Tierno summarizes the key elements of successful drama. Tierno calls Aristotle the first movie story analyst and explains what Aristotle recognized as "timeless universal truths about dramatic storytelling."[52] Tierno introduces us to Aristotle's first rule of storytelling: "Say what the story demands."[53] To give that concept substance, Tierno introduces the "action-idea" — the essence of Aristotle's *Poetics*.

Aristotle's action-idea is that simple idea of the protagonist's physical goal that holds the audience's attention through to the end. Another term for the action-idea might be "high-concept" — a plot

---

[52] Tierno, p. xix.
[53] Tierno, p. 1.

idea that can be described in a few words and generate in the hearer an emotional, if not visceral, reaction. *Jaws* is about "stopping a killer shark."[54] Simple. Emotional. A whole movie in that one short line.

The goal of the storyteller is to take the audience through an emotional and psychological journey that reveals a poignant truth about the human experience. Such journeys are cathartic and create, with the audience, a deep resonance. But, as Tierno explains, to make a whole movie about such a simple action-idea demands that the protagonist, in trying to fulfill the action-idea, must make a *"moral choice."*[55]

When we see the protagonist struggle with the difficulty of making a tough decision we identify with that character and try to make the choice for him. Ultimately, such choices are difficult because they deal with dilemmas involving unclear moral rights and wrongs. If the protagonist makes one decision, the consequences might have some good involved, but the risk of something bad happening is also a possibility.

Tierno also talks about the unity of action or "through line" that, if the filmmaker does it right, brings all the disparately separate occurrences in the movie around *one subject* and ties them together in a logical progression of cause and effect, from beginning to end. Aristotle says the drama must be about "a single, and not a double issue."[56] That is, all the characters struggle with the same thing, but in different ways. In *American Beauty* all the characters are seeking to embrace a beauty that eludes them. And throughout *American Beauty* each of the characters make moral decisions that affect how they are able to perceive and experience that beauty.

By showing us in actionable events how each character seeks out what they perceive as beautiful (Lester lusts for Angela, Janey falls for Ricky, Carol makes it with Buddy, and Colonel Fitz makes a pass at Lester), the filmmakers take an idea and make it visible, and allow us to derive the whole movie's theme through the individual parts.

Tierno comments about *The Breakfast Club*: "In every molecule of the story you can sense the simple ACTION-IDEA because the plot is evoked in every scene." That is something my own research revealed: For a movie to succeed the Moral Premise must be consistently evident in every scene and each main characters' arc. "The

---

[54] Tierno, p. 3.
[55] Tierno, p. 4.
[56] Tierno, p. 25.

whole is always in each of the parts."[57] In the context of the Moral Premise every scene must reflect the Moral Premise, as should every character arc, as should the set design, as should... everything else. The parts reinforce the whole, and every part of the movie's theme is tested, reflected, and articulated in each individual scene. "*All the action* that brings change in the story must raise the central moral question.... The audience *wants* to see right and wrong addressed, because everyone feels that this gets at the heart of what it is to be human."[58]

This is the same things as Lajos Egri's "premise," and Robert McKee's "controlling-idea" — that is, the Moral Premise. It is the Moral Premise that causes the action or the plot to move forward to its inevitable conclusion. And since we in the audience see the hero go through a well-spring of actions and decisions that challenge and even compromise his journey, we root for him to make the *right* decision. If the filmmakers have done their job, we have a window to the protagonist's mind, and our involvement in the story turns on the protagonist's ability to make the right moral decision that moves the plot and story into a direction we'd like to see. The moral thought is the *cause*, the plot is the *effect*. And it is those moral thoughts, decisions, and actions that create in us an emotional feeling about the virtues and vices with which the protagonist struggles.

Later in Chapter 8 — Step 1, when I ask you to select a virtue, and then in Chapter 9 — Step 2 when you select an opposing vice, you must pick a virtue and vice that are true. Not just true to you, but true to your audience as well. Movies create emotional journeys and cathartic endings, not by presenting *new* moral perspectives or truth, but by putting the characters through "archetypical experiences" that are psychologically identical to the audience's own.[59] The physical plot or explicit premise may be false, as in *Galaxy Quest* (aliens recruiting actors to save the universe), but the psychological or implicit premises are true (our universal call to duty, courage and responsibility).

"That's why it's important to build actions on 'universals' — to substantiate universal truths about the human condition through the action of the plot," writes Tierno.[60] When we present truths in new

---

[57] Tierno, p. 34-35.
[58] Tierno, p. 32-72.
[59] Tierno, p. 109.
[60] Tierno, p. 109.

ways, we cause our audience to remember that truth, which may have come to them in an entirely different situation. But being reminded of it in a fresh way triggers the "Ah, ha!"

The way I like to think about this is that the explicit premise becomes the metaphor or myth for the psychological or Moral Premise upon which the whole story is based. We watch a physical story about a psychological truth and our recognition of that truth produces in us an emotional and visceral clarity about life and its meaning. This is an absolutely crucial requirement of successful movies. That is why in Part II we begin with the end in mind, or the underlying universal truth, and on that we build the plot. Or, we might start with an intriguing physical plot, and before too much time passes, discover what universal moral truth the story is really about. In this way, the individual plot elements will reinforce in an implicit, subtle, and even subliminal way what the movie is really about, and the parts of the movie will indeed become the whole.

MICHAEL HAUGE'S *THEME*

Earlier, we touched on Michael Hauge's *Writing Screenplays That Sell* and what he says about *theme*. But there's something to say here as well. Theme, as Hauge defines it, is very similar to the Moral Premise. In Chapter 5, I'll demonstrate how a movie's theme is actually only one-half of a Moral Premise; but for the sake of the immediate discussion let's assume that the Moral Premise and theme are the same.

For Hauge, the greatness of American movies is that they can be wonderfully entertaining in terms of the protagonist's outer motivation and yet, underneath the action, appeal to audiences with universal truths. He writes: "This underlying level of morality is explored through the film's theme. Theme is the universal statement the movie makes about the human condition... it applies to any individual in the audience."[61]

First, note that Hauge implies that the theme is a *universal moral truth*. Second, note this reference to audience appeal. These two combine to form a very significant aspect of stories that resonate with

---

[61] Hauge, pp.74-84.

audiences.[62] Consider the physical quest of the protagonist, Harry S. Stamper, in *Armageddon*. Harry's physical goal is to land on an Earth-threatening asteroid and blow it up. While landing on asteroids, let alone blowing them up, is not a universal theme (not many of us have experienced such an adventure), the importance of the underlying themes the movie explores (sacrificial love, honor, protecting mankind), are universal moral truths that apply to all human beings, in all places, throughout time.

I can also accept Hauge's suggestion that a screenwriter should start with the protagonist's outer motivation[63] and not delve into the story's theme (or inner journey) until the outer story is fleshed out. Hauge believes that the theme should not be investigated until the second or third draft of the script. His fear is that the theme will be superimposed on your story in such an artificial way that it will destroy the all-important outer motivation and plot... becoming a tacky message film. That's a concern I share.

But I disagree that you should wait for the second or third draft of the *script*. A proactive approach would be to develop the protagonist's outer motivation in the first draft of the story outline and *treat-*

William Wallace's Act 2 Moment of Grace in *Braveheart*. After being knighted by the Scottish nobles, Wallace tells them: "There is a difference between us. You think the people of this country exist to provide you with position. I think your position exists to provide those people with freedom. And I go to make sure that they have it." ©1995, Paramount Home Video

---

[62] See Chapter 6 on Identification and the Moral Premise.

[63] To clarify terms, Hauge's outer motivation for the protagonist is the same thing as my explicit premise — the protagonist's physical goal.

ment. Then you can make the Moral Premise connection (or theme connection) during the second and third draft of the *treatment*. As I describe later, so much of the main character's motivation hinges on the Moral Premise that to wait even until after a first draft of the script will require considerable and unnecessary rework.

If Hauge is right that the *cornerstone* of any good screenplay is the main character's outer motivation, then the Moral Premise is the *engraving* on the cornerstone — telling us why the cornerstone is there. The outer and inner motivations are inextricably linked, because the outer motivation is the physical metaphor for the inner motivation. Until we know *why* the cornerstone is there, we have no idea *how* to tell the story in a way that is consistently about one single, universal idea.

SYD FIELD'S *INTERIOR LIFE*

Syd Field's *Screenplay: The Foundations of Screenwriting* provides us with a different perspective and a subsequent problem that, I believe, has generated its fair share of writer's block and perpetual confusion.

I want to start by saying that I do respect Field's book in many ways. He gets a great deal right; and well he should, having been in the position for years of helping to select hundreds of scripts and watching their success or failure at the box office. But where Field falls short is in the creative process of devising the stories that end up as scripts. There are three aspects of the writing process that Field discusses that are sure to slow down the process; they are *backstory*, *context*, and *point of view*. Please stick with me through this discussion. It may seem like it doesn't have much to do with the Moral Premise, but it does. The method I explain later is intended to help you, as a writer, determine in a consistent, logical manner your character's backstory, context, and point of view.

As you know, it is important for a writer to understand his characters so thoroughly that their current actions come naturally from the multiple dimensions of who they are. Field, however, approaches the decisions about a character's backstory, context, and point of view through a door I think no writer should enter. Let me explain, and then afterwards I'll contrast Field's approach with Egri's and tie in the centrality of the Moral Premise.

Field's "Backstory"

Field directs the writer to first "establish your main character" and write a detailed biography of the character's prior life, in order to know the character's interior motivation for the outer story that begins with the screenplay. This is good. In Chapter 3 of his book Field provides a slew of questions to ask yourself about your character. Here are a few of them:

> Start with the *interior* life. Is your character male or female? If male, how old is he when the story begins? Where does he live?... What kind of childhood did he have?... What kind of child was he? Outgoing, an extrovert; or studious, an intro-vert?... What does your character do for a living?... Is your main character single, widowed, married, separated, or divorced?... What does your character do when he or she is by himself? What is the *need* of your character? What does he or she want in your screenplay? *Define the need of your character.*[64]

Good questions. They need answers. But Field offers no hints about how these questions can be answered in a way that logically develops the story. It appears as if *any* answers would do, and it's true... you're free to be wildly, even randomly creative. Many writers, myself included, have spent days answering Field's questions, making up stuff that sounds interesting, hip, and inventive. At the end of the day, you look in the bedroom mirror and proudly proclaim, "Hey, isn't this great? I'm a writer!"

But one morning your pillow feels suspiciously like someone filled it with bricks. Knowing no fear, you splash water on your face, go to your writing corner, apply rear-end to chair (Rule No. 1), power up your word processor, call up your script file, and, placing fingers above the keyboard, you wait for the inspiration that you just know will cascade great ideas down upon you and the keyboard... and... and... nothing. Nothing! The flashing cursor is putting you to sleep.

Perhaps a softer pillow on the chair?

Still... nothing.

---

[64] Field, pp. 28-30 (Field's Italics).

A drive in the car... to Vegas and back. "Hey, that was fun."
Back at the computer. Another pillow?
Blank.
Suddenly, all those hot backstory ideas are as cold as a waterbed filled with dry ice.
Writer's block!
But why after all that backstory work?
The reason is that all those nifty answers have little or nothing to do with the drama of your story, although they should have everything to do with it. "But," you whimper, "I want to keep those wild and crazy ideas. They're so cool." So, you desperately try to cram them into your story. But they don't fit. The bricks wear holes in the pillowcase, and your waterbed looks like the iceberg that sank the *Titanic*.[65]

FIELD'S "CONTEXT"

Field's second step is to create a *context* for the "*idea* of a person, as it exists in scrambled, fragmented form, and make him or her into a living, flesh-and-blood person." Those are his words — *scrambled* and *fragmented* — not mine. He writes, "define the need of your character" and in the process give that character "a point of view and an attitude." Again, I wonder. What guides the writer's decisions to choose a need, a point of view, or an attitude?[66]

To me, this is backwards. If writers generally follow this process, it may explain why so many scripts go through 20 rewrites before they get made... if they get made at all. Granted, the backstory, in chronological story-time, comes before the screenplay's story. But to the writer who is creating a character, it is the backstory that gives motivation, drive, force to the spine of the screenplay. Until the writer has a fairly good idea what the story is really about he can't write the backstory that gives drive and purpose to his musings. Yet, if the writer has some inkling of the Moral Premise, there is a logical and efficient way to write the character's backstory. If you know the story's Moral

---

[65] Andrew Horton does something similar in *Writing the Character-Centered Screenplay* on pages 83-85, with little more advice than Field provides about how to answer the litany of personality and backstory questions. Horton's instructions to the writer are no better than Field's. Horton writes: "Trust your gut reactions... as to how they [the characters] came to be that way."
[66] "Need" is the right concept, not ""want." But Field brings up *need* too late and doesn't explain its psychological importance.

Premise and the character's relation to it, you can efficiently answer all of Field's questions in relatively quick order and end up with a multi-dimensional, fully motivated, and conflicted character.

Now, in all fairness, I suspect that there is an unspoken assumption on Field's part that the aspiring screenwriter already knows the character's backstory and that answering the litany of questions is just a way to flesh it out and help make it all cogent and consistent. In other words, Field may be assuming that the aspiring writer will have massaged the story in his or her mind before actually putting a word to paper. Thus, the answers come easy and not in a scrambled or fragmented way. But it was Field who used the terms "scrambled and fragmented" and that is what many writers that read his book assume. I did and I wasted many weeks chipping away at my petrified writer's block.

Field's process asks the writer to create an interesting character and *then, from* the character's quirks, dig out a story that an audience might find interesting. As I suggest later on, the opposite would be much more efficient.

Field's "Point of View"

Field tells the aspiring writer to make a detailed assessment of his main character and what drives that protagonist to make decisions. This is an excellent suggestion, but Field never tells the writer *how* to do that precisely, But he does offer what I think is some misleading advice.

When discussing the character's point of view, Field makes the observation that the point of view of a criminal will be different from a cop, or the point of view of a rich man will be different than that of a poor man. But when discussing the character's behavior Field writes:

> If you reach a point in your screenplay where you don't know what your characters will do in a certain situation, go into your own life and find out what you would do in a similar situation. You're the best source material you have. Exercise it. If you created the problem, you can solve it.[67]

[67] Field, p. 40.

No wonder writers can be confused and misdirected. If I'm a well-read, disciplined, law-abiding citizen... albeit a working writer on the edge of poverty... it is not likely that I am the best source material for a character who's illiterate, lazy, and a career loan shark. Now it is true that as a writer I have to imagine myself as an illiterate crook to write about one, but hopefully I will have researched such a lifestyle before I try to imagine it out of my *own* much different experience.

Field then describes what has been repeated in dozens of places in other books on writing in various genres. It's advice that has some merit if you know where the story is going. But at this early stage, Field's advice illustrates yet another reason why it may take followers of his strategy years and dozens of drafts to get a good screenplay structured. He writes:

> When you are in the writing process you will find it will take you anywhere from 20 to 50 pages before your characters start talking to you, telling you what *they* want to *do* and *say*. Once you've made contact, and established a connection with your people, they'll take over. Let them...[68]

God help the writer who follows this advice... if even God could. Field writes about the importance of knowing your character so you can write intelligently about him or her. But, suppose by this time you have your character's backstory all documented, you know this guy or gal intimately, and now you begin to let the character tell the story, as Field suggests. What if your character doesn't want to tell *your* story but has one of his or her own? Do you go off and give wings to your *character's* muse? Well, it might be fun, and it might be interesting. But it will also be very inefficient... and chances are you'll not end up with something useable. In such a case, go directly to your on-line stock trader, buy a stake in a paper company, and start counting the drafts and reams of paper you use. You'll be farther along.

FIELD VS. EGRI

Now let's contrast Field's approach to Egri's.

In Egri's chapter on *Character* the first section is subtitled *Bone*

---

[68] Field, p. 41.

Structure. In this section he provides an outline of the things a writer needs to know about a character in order to make that character come alive dimensionally. He suggests 27 categories in three dimensions — physiology, sociology, and psychology.[69] Field's questions and Egri's bone structure outline are very similar and serve the same purpose — they intend to help writers be thoroughly informed about the characters whose lives are being dramatized.

The difference between the two is that Field makes no attempt to connect the answers of the character questions to the character's actions in the story... or the Moral Premise. But Egri does. Egri sets up and elucidates his bone structure beginning with the first paragraph of the chapter.

> In the previous chapter we showed why [the moral] premise is necessary as the first step in writing a good play.... If we wish to understand the action of any individual, we must look at the motivation which compels him to act as he does... [the] reasons for human conduct... trace his motivation to its source... know his personal premise, and its motivation.... Anything that happens in your play must come directly from the characters you have chosen to prove your premise, and they must be characters strong enough to prove the premise without forcing.[70]

 Egri never says it as directly as I would like, but his intent is clear: *Create a characters' backstory that will compel them to play out the plot of your tale in a naturally unfolding drama and prove the story's Moral Premise.*

OTHER AUTHORS

Although time and space do not allow extensive discussion, there are other helpful authors who point to the Moral Premise in their books. In Christopher Vogler's *The Writer's Journey* the Moral Premise comes in the form of the Elixir that the hero brings back to the Ordinary World. Although Vogler and his mentor, Joseph Campbell, broaden

---

[69] Field, pp. 36-37.
[70] Field, pp. 32-43.

the concept of the elixir to include physical objects, those objects nonetheless are metaphors of what Vogler calls "the lesson learned... with the power to heal a wounded land... the fruits of our journey... [that] brings deep healing, wellness, and wholeness to our world"[71] and what Campbell means when the hero must return to his community with the "life-transmuting trophy... the runes of wisdom, the Golden Fleece, or his sleeping princess."[72]

In James Bonnet's *Stealing Fire from the Gods* the Moral Premise is "The Hidden Truth" of the "story focus" that characters seek in their "pursuit of some important value... and by the avoidance of their opposites."[73] This structure (seeking something of value while avoiding the opposite) is precisely how the Moral Premise statement should be constructed, as I explain in Chapter 5.

Linda Seger's *Making a Good Script Great* suggests that the writer can connect with the audience by raising the *stakes* in the story by jeopardizing the characters' psychological *needs* (as opposed to physical *wants*). In the process, Seger reminds us that the protagonist must transform and change, which is exactly what the Moral Premise demands of a story.[74]

David Trottier in *The Screenwriter's Bible* tells us that although the central character has a conscious goal "beneath it all looms a great unconscious *need... the heart of the story* or the *emotional through-line*,"[75] i.e. the Moral Premise.

Although Lew Hunter in Screenwriting 434 spends little more than a page on the topic, he cites Lajos Egri, the importance of theme, and Egri's premise. In Hunter's subsection called "What's It Really About" he quotes UCLA professor Howard Suber: "What the film is about is not the plot," then gives homage to Egri and reinforces how the [moral] premise and every other part of the film must "blend into a harmonious whole" that is universally true to the audience.[76]

---

[71] Vogler, pp 221-235.

[72] Campbell, p. 179.

[73] Bonnett, p. 51, 128.

[74] Seger, pp. 128-129.

[75] Trottier, p. 24-25, ff.

[76] Hunter, p. 67-68.

Andrew Horton, in *Writing the Character-Centered Screenplay*, infers the Moral Premise in his Character Note #3: "In the Character-centered script, we and the characters are confronted with difficult and often contradictory moral choices."[77] Note Horton's inclusion of the audience "we" along with the "characters." That points to the importance of the audience's moral identification with the characters.

Finally, in Dona Cooper's *Writing Great Screenplays for Film and TV*, the Moral Premise is her "Dramatic Equation." Cooper explains the Moral Premise concept very clearly, although she writes only about a half page:

> The dramatic equation of a story is its message or statement of values. Boiled down to its essence, your script conveys the message "this person plus this change inevitably equals this outcome." Like an algebraic equation, the internal dynamics of a story must add up and make sense.... The internal logic behind the series of changes must still hold up in order for the audience to feel a sense of clarity and completion. Viewers may not be conscious of the equation; in fact, they usually aren't unless they try to articulate their thoughts

Helen tells her husband, Bob, the secret of the moral premise in *The Incredibles*: "If we were to work together you won't have to be [strong enough by yourself]... Hey, we're superheroes [we're a family]." ©2005 Disney/Pixar

[77] Horton, p. 7.

about the film. If they do, you may be surprised just how clearly viewers register the central statement of your film.[78]

The formal research that I conducted from 1994 to 1998, and which I continue informally today, provides strong evidence for Cooper's conclusions. In brief, I discovered that there was a direct correlation between the consistency and truth of a film's Moral Premise and its success at the box office. The consistency portion of that discovery is what Cooper means when she writes, "the internal dynamics of the story must add up and make sense." Audiences do not always have a conscious awareness of a film's Moral Premise, but their connection with the film as a whole depends on it.

Suffice it to say, the concept of the Moral Premise is nearly ubiquitous — it's everywhere. And the reason is simple; regardless of how the screenwriter goes about crafting tales, the Moral Premise is at the natural root of all good storytelling, especially at the movies. And that "naturalness" is what the next chapter is all about.

---

[78] Cooper, p 77.

EXERCISES

1. Create a list of different books on writing. Contrast and compare how each author refers to moral themes and premises.

2. Describe how a writer can use Field's backstory questions to construct a character's motivation that is consistent and clear.

3. Select a single value from the lists in Chapter I, or one of your own. Describe three backstory anecdotes in a character's life that would cause that value to be evident in a character's screen life. Your description could form the basis of a treatment for a short film.

4. Select a favorite movie character and then answer Egri's backstory questions about that character. Explain how that character's values were derived from their backstory.

STORYTELLING'S
NATURAL LAW AND PROCESSES

4

A NATURAL LAW

Good, well-structured stories attract us because there is something natural about them, like taking a breath of fresh air or walking with the aid of gravity's downward pull. We are psychologically pulled into good stories because there is something inherent in their structure that we identify as a natural part of how the universe works. Good stories tell us something that rings true about our experience as human beings.

Although we do not fully understand certain laws of physics and psychology, we know that some at least are true. We come to trust them. If we step off a cliff we will fall until we hit the ground. If we lie to friends and they find out, they will trust us less in the future. Even if we are not caught in our lie we will not trust ourselves as easily. In all this there is a cause and effect that we can naturally expect. When tectonic plates grind against each other there are earthquakes, tsunamis, and other *physical* consequences. When personalities grind against each other there are arguments, waves of mistrust, and other *psychological* consequences. As writers, we may not always understand the natural laws of storytelling, but we can understand that for every action there will be a natural reaction... and for every cause there is a natural effect.

No man-made laws of government or religion create such natural laws. Laws written by religious institutions, governments, or scientific academies simply attempt to codify what the legislators believe are naturally true. Such natural laws are just there, built into the physical universe and into our collective psychological conscience.[79]

---

[79] Living in compliance with nature brings safety and harmony, living in defiance of nature brings danger and discord. Governments typically don't say such things explicitly, but the foundation of all laws, especially the function of judicial systems, is to judge whether or not laws are "fair" or "just" and whether or not the judgment fits the crime. The concepts of "fairness" and "justice" are synonymous with naturalness. Such a system of evaluation is an attempt to discern and put into place societal rules that naturally bring harmony between humans, and between humans and nature. Likewise, Catholic theology teaches that its doctrines are attempts at explaining what is naturally true in the physical and psychological realms. That is why the Catholic Church will often say that it does not have the authority to change a teaching... i.e. they cannot change natural law.

On the other hand, although mankind did not need Newton to formulate the mathematical formula for the force of gravity to prove its truth, writing out the law as best we understand it does help us live in harmony with nature more readily, effectively, and safety... as we design roller coasters, airplanes, buildings, or water towers. Just as most of us do not need a law of government to tell us that lying, theft, or murder are wrong, or that there may be some natural consequence after the fact, writing out the law and promising a more ready punishment helps to secure an orderly society.[80]

In essence, that is what this book is attempting to do — to explain one of the natural laws of storytelling — the natural law of the Moral Premise. With that, let me introduce the form of the Moral Premise, its natural law, and three corollaries. When applied together they give a film the best possible foundation for box office success.

General Form of the Moral Premise
Vice leads to undesirable consequences;
but Virtue leads to desirable consequences.

Natural Law of the Moral Premise
A story's consistent application of a true Moral Premise
improves success.

Corollary A
A story's inconsistent application of a true Moral Premise
will lead to a film's demise.

Corollary B
Any application of a false Moral Premise
will lead to a film's demise.

Corollary C
The target audience determines the truth of the Moral Premise.

These corollaries are explained in detail later in the text so I will not belabor them at this point, except for one comment about Corollary C. The most successful movies are about universal truths that apply to all people, in all places, throughout all history. But that is not to say

---

[80] $Fg = (G M_1 M_2) / D^2$ – where M1 and M2 are the masses of the objects, D is the distance between the centers of the two objects, and G is a number called Newton's Universal Constant of Gravitation.

Just before his release, Rubin Carter reflects with Lesra on his journey and the moral premise in *The Hurricane*: "Hate put me in prison. Love's gonna bust me out." ©2000, Universal Studios

that a movie cannot be successful when its Moral Premise is targeted at a particular audience who hold to moral beliefs that are not universal. Such a story, aimed at a niche audience, may find success, but its success will always be much more limited than if the Moral Premise was truly universal.

To the extent that I'm correct and to the extent that you disregard this law, your stories will be about things unnatural and negative consequences at the box office will result. But to the extent that I'm correct and to the extent that you follow the law of the Moral Premise, your stories will be more likely to be accepted by mass audiences with positive box office results.

These rules surrounding the Moral Premise are useful. They explain what has been here for millennia, and how to tap into this naturally occurring phenomenon to write successful stories.

NATURAL PROCESSES

I'm sure it's true that many of the successful stories of our time are created without any conscious knowledge about the Moral Premise's natural law. So, it's fair to ask: How do those stories get written without the writers literally and consciously being aware of what a Moral Premise is, or its rules of usage?

First, I think the fact that successful stories are continually written about predictable and recurring patterns of good and evil, and cause and effect, is evidence enough that there is a natural law of story telling. Second, explaining the law and providing a way to access it doesn't mean the law can't be accessed in some other way. Successful writers do not need to understand the rules of story writing to be successful, anymore than a young child needs to understand the dynamic stability laws of physics when they learn to walk. Although I think a writer is better off knowing what the rules are, whereas dynamic stability only matters to engineers who want to make robots walk on two legs.

As I've admitted, Part II leans toward a left-brain kind of process as one way to follow this natural law process. But in reality, for many creative tasks, the right brain is able to do just fine all by itself... thank you very much. Okay, I don't really believe the right brain can operate by itself. But such is the marginalizing of left-brain processes that one might conclude that any linear process is bereft of originality. Nonetheless, many Hollywood writers and other artists come up with great works in organic, nonlinear ways. Let me describe a few of those ways to you in an effort to make a point that the left-brain and linear processes are only as good as the right-brain and global processes allow.

Trial and Revision

Successful writers can connect with a story's true Moral Premise by trial and revision. I write analytical essays about films and occasionally have the opportunity to interview writers, directors, or producers. One writer, with a long list of released movies behind his name, finally got the chance to direct and co-produce one of his scripts with major stars. When I saw the film, I thought the story was very well structured and grounded in a clear Moral Premise. The project had the distinct flair of an "independent film," and although it was never given good distribution, it garnered significant critical acclaim. It was thoughtful, creative, and everything about the film fit neatly around the story's Moral Premise. The film was Ed Solomon's *Levity* with Billy Bob Thornton, Morgan Freeman, and Kirsten Durst.

When I interviewed Ed I discovered he was totally unaware of the movie's Moral Premise, or that each of the characters' arcs, the setting, the conflict, and much of the dialogue has a systemic, focused essence that, in my opinion, made the film work on numerous levels. I wrote an essay about this that was published and sent Ed a copy. *Levity's* Moral Premise could be stated this way: *"Truth leads to levity, but deception leads to despair."* Everything in the movie pointed to this truth: The plot, the physical and psychological arcs of each of the main characters, special effects, art direction, camera positions and staging, lighting, and even the direction of the background extras. Ed's first reaction to my essay was surprise, and delight that everything I saw in the movie was actually there. Ed claimed he did not consciously intend for the elements that glued the story together to be there. But he readily acknowledged that they were.

As we dialogued by email over the following weeks, it became clear that the process he followed in writing his directing debut could be described as *trial and revision*. He would write a draft and send it to some of his friends, or to potential actors such as Freeman. Upon receiving their feedback he would rewrite the script. This went on over a number of drafts and years, as I recall. His readers would identify something that needed attention... Ed would make revisions... and then send it out again. More suggestions, more revisions... and in this way the story's structure slowly took shape. Eventually his screenplay hit a strong enough resonance with Freeman and Thornton that *Levity* got made.

After watching *Levity* several times, and talking to Ed, I'm convinced that had he been able to figure out what the story was *really* about beforehand, his writing would have hit a resonance with actors, producers, and distribution more easily. His friends had a subconscious sense, as he does, of what works and what doesn't. And over time, and by trial and revision, this sense created a cogent film with a strong and consistently applied true Moral Premise that was received well.[81]

---

[81] *Levity* never received the distribution it deserved. I suspect this was because distributors did not understand the film's Moral Premise and how to leverage what the movie was really about to the right market.

Instinct & Osmosis

Writers also create stories with true Moral Premises through instinct. For about a year I worked with another talented writer in Hollywood, Douglas Lloyd McIntosh, who has written and produced scripts for Steven Spielberg, Michael Mann, and Francis Ford Coppola. Doug and I labored for months writing 2,000-word synopses for a slate of screenplays my company wanted to develop. Doug's a wonderful guy to work with and he makes a fabulous cinnamon-laced tea! But our methods were quite different and at times frustrating for both of us.

When I tried to focus our decision-making process around Egri's premise theories or the developing ideas that eventually made it into this book, Doug would ask me not to rush, fearing that my process was too rigid and that in his words, "somebody like me had to pull you back from the brink." Although he also felt that "our separate approaches complemented each other very well, and we each brought concerns to the table that resulted in better stories precisely because we were coming at them from somewhat different directions."[82]

Doug wanted to "discover" and "get to know" the character first, before we made any decisions about the character's actions. I wanted to know the character's psychological or backstory motivation first. We were just wired differently, I concluded. In a word, Doug's process was *instinctual*. He has the ability to experience the lives of his fictional characters in a gestalt[83] way that I could not do. His fear in working with me was that "overdependence on rules of story construction... limits creativity and can lead to thin, two-dimensional, and unconvincing characters." His concern is a valid one to be sure.

But on retrospect, Doug's good instinct for story came from a very disciplined lifetime of exposure to stories. Doug's apartment near Westwood is crammed with a vast array of meticulously shelved books with new library covers — the fruits of thousands of hours of reading. For decades Doug has read at least one book a week... both

---

[82] Douglas Lloyd McIntosh, personal communication, February 10, 2005.

[83] Gestalt processes require that the "whole" of the entity be studied and that the whole cannot be known by studying its individual parts. My way of thinking was to study the parts and see how they might fit together, but instinctual thinkers sense the whole from the onset. That is real talent.

[84] Douglas Bulka, personal communication, March 17, 2005.

fiction and non-fiction. His collection dwarfs that of a small town library, and since there is no more wall space where he lives, the librarians in Santa Monica have gotten to know him well.

Additionally, as a young boy he tried to see seven movies every week. That's one feature every day (!), a rate that did not slack off until he was over forty. He wrote me about this:

> Once when I was at the NYU film school, Mike Clark and I (he's now the chief film critic for *USA Today*) set the all-time record with eight movies in a single day! We started out at eight in the morning at the Museum of Modern Art, moved to Radio City for the 10 or 11 a.m., caught the subway down-town for a couple of double features, and wound up back at his apartment for a couple of 16 mm films, including a gor-geous color print of Cecil B. DeMille's *Reap the Wild Wind*, which is the only title I remember out of the crazy day.

Was Doug's "instinct" for a good story something he was born with? He doesn't think so, but rather it's the product of exposing himself literally to "thousands of stories, good, bad, and indifferent." In other words, *instinct* for a story that works (and its Moral Premise) can be acquired through *osmosis* — immersion into the art.

It Comes Naturally

Finding true Moral Premises also comes naturally to some writers. Although they may not always be able to articulate it, they have an inherent understanding of human nature and natural law. They know how things are supposed to work, just like a child prodigy can hear a piano melody and play it correctly the first time through.

I filmed a 17-year-old young man a month ago who has mastered classical piano, at least to my hearing. It is amazing to see this young man's fingers fly over the keys, faster than my eyes can follow. With no visible hesitation he can play seemingly for hours with no music. He's the musical pride of his high school having placed first in a number of state competitions. I assumed Jonathan Misch had been taking lessons and playing since he was five or six years old. But, when

I asked, he told me he had wanted to play since he was five or six, but for family reasons he was unable to take lessons until he was 13, just four years ago. The deciding factor for his mother, who had to foot the bill, was when they visited a cousin who had been taking piano lessons for years, and who had struggled for months to learn how to play this one particular composition. John wanted to try... and before he and his mom returned home, about 30 minutes later, John had learned to play the entire piece, amazing everyone.

Some individuals discover that they are drawn to a particular subject or career because they not only find it easier than anything else in their experience, but because their fascination continually motivates them to get out of bed every morning the rest of their lives. Some people do it just because they can... easily, wonderfully, and naturally. It's in their DNA.

An acquaintance of mine who is a nationally exhibited artist recently described his decision during his first year of university to change from pre-med studies to art history. He wrote me:

> I worked so hard at organic chemistry and just could not get any of the knowledge to stick. That first semester, I also took an elective course in art history. Unlike the chemistry course, I could read material about art history once and it made sense. I found myself completely engrossed while studying it, and still am today. It revealed itself to me as if I was revisiting a life-long friend for the first time after a very long bout with amnesia. It just felt right. With the chemistry or math courses, I always felt I had to force or beat the information into my head. So I applied to art school.[84]

Today, Douglas Bulka is a nationally exhibited artist and is also employed at one of the country's major art museums. He found what came natural to him and succeeded in pursuing it.

Reading about Stephen King's career, especially during his early years of poverty, seems to paint a similar picture — he too became engrossed in his art, unable to do anything else with equal passion or confidence. His writing came to him and motivated him *naturally*.

---

[84] Douglas Bulka, personal communication, March 17, 2005.

The terminator clarifies the moral premise in *Terminator 2*: "SARAH: It's over. TERMINATOR: No There's one more chip... (he points to his head)... and it must be destroyed also." ©1991, Artisan Home Entertainment

Talent

Recognizing and incorporating the true Moral Premise in a story is also one of the outcomes of raw *talent*. We all know what "talent" is when we see it. Or we should. We almost worship those people that act, sing, dance, or mesmerize us with keyboards or brush. Talent oozes from their chords, pores, and palettes. I was recently at a surprise birthday party near Hollywood for a beautiful singer, composer, actress, artist, and dancer. Yes, she does it all well. Tatiana Cameron is extremely talented in the arts while her husband, Matt, is just as talented at taking care of business and the kids, except he still needs some help with the breastfeeding. It works well for them. But at this party there were a number of their friends whom, it seemed, could all play the piano while their backs were turned toward it. (The upright piano was pushed against a wall and to make eye contact each guest performer had to sit sidesaddle on the piano bench, hands on the keyboard, with face turned toward the crowd.) Tatiana's friends could play and sing seemingly anything, from memory, and do it in the appropriate style and genre of the original artist. It was a grand night that went on, and on, and on. Talent was everywhere. They would say they work hard at it, but we know it's more natural for them than if we were to ever try.

Perseverance & Perspiration

Digging out the true Moral Premise of a story can also be the product of *perseverance* and *perspiration*. Take someone like Lance Armstrong... not a writer, but perhaps some writers can learn about perseverance from watching Lance pedal up the steep hill outside their writing hovel. Yes, watching Lance pedal a bicycle up the side of the French Alps (or Laurel Canyon Boulevard) is exhilarating, and, yes, he is one of the few men with the physical capacity to excel in the sport of cycling. But having the genes isn't enough. Lance persevered through pain, cancer, agony, and years of hard discipline. The yellow LIVE-STRONG wristband on the arms of millions of his fans is a reminder to perseverance. Lance writes:

> Yellow wakes me up in the morning.
> Yellow gets me on the bike every day.
> Yellow has taught me the true meaning of sacrifice.
> Yellow makes me suffer.
> Yellow is the reason I'm here.

Perseverance is nothing without sacrifice, and perspiration is nothing without pain. It isn't enough to have the right DNA, a good competitor has to persevere through the pain of it all. Lance's train-ing only took effect because he persevered and perspired through the winter months when his competitors, by their own admission, were downing pints of ale in neighborhood pubs. Lance discovered he was made to naturally persevere and he capitalized on it.

The same is true of some writers, and other great creators. "Genius is one percent inspiration and ninety-nine per cent per-spiration," said Thomas Edison. Some successful writers may not have what it takes naturally, but many have made the grade through perseverance and perspiration.

⤸

Each of the individuals I've just told you about are inspirations. They tell us things can be done, in a variety of natural ways. They prove to us that there are many ways to get the job done. I don't claim that what follows is the only way or the best way. Again, what matters is not the process you follow but the results you get — a true Moral Premise imbued into every aspect of your story and film. The natural goal.

Okay, enough of the history, theory, and my attempts at inspiration. Let's get down to the nuts and bolts of the Moral Premise, which is what the next chapter is about. Remember, even if the detailed process isn't for you, by studying what follows you'll catch a glimpse, or perhaps a strong vision, of how the Moral Premise can naturally tie everything about your film together, and how you might, in your unique way, write a great story and make a wonderfully successful film.

EXERCISES

1. Explain in your own words what this chapter describes as a natural law of storytelling.

2. Describe four reasons or nonlinear techniques that successful writers might use to create a story that connects with audiences.

3. Research the writing life of a published narrative author or writer, and write a short essay about how that writer formulates and structures stories (e.g. James A. Michener's *Writer's Handbook*).

4. Examine writings on the creative process or artist endeavors and list the ways other authors suggest an artist can create works that connect with audiences (e.g. Guy Claxton's *Hare Brain Tortoise Mind*; Twyla Tharp's *The Creative Habit: Learn It and Use It for Life*; Rudolf Flesch's *The Art of Clear Thinking*; Doug Hall's *Jump Start Your Brain*; Tony Buzan's *Using Both Sides of Our Brain*; Alex Osborn's *Applied Imagination*; and Martin Gardner's *aha! Insight*.

STRUCTURE OF THE MORAL PREMISE

5

FORM OF THE MORAL PREMISE

While the Moral Premise can be summarized or short-handed in a number of ways, there is a form that is comprehensive and useful. It is comprised of four parts: a virtue, a vice, desirable consequences (success), and undesirable consequences (defeat). These four parts can be used to create a statement that describes precisely what a movie is really about, on both physical and psychological levels. This is the formal structure of a Moral Premise:

> [Vice] leads to [defeat], but
> [Virtue] leads to [success].

Here are two examples. *City Slickers'* Moral Premise can be expressed:

> *Sel<u>fish</u>ness leads to sadness and frowns, but*
> *Sel<u>fless</u>ness leads to happiness and smiles.*

Die Hard's Moral Premise can be expressed:

> *Covetous hatred leads to death and destruction, but*
> *Sacrificial love leads to life and celebration.*

As I will describe later, there are subtle differences in how this formula can be stated, but the essential relationships between the four parts never changes.

THEMES VS. MORAL PREMISES

Shorthand descriptions of the Moral Premise are often referred to as a movie's theme. For instance, *Die Hard's* theme can be stated as one-half of the Moral Premise:

> *Covetous hatred leads to death and destruction.*

or

> *Sacrificial love leads to life and celebration.*

More poetic forms of the theme also work. We can say *Die Hard* is about how...

> *...true love dies hard*
> *...a vulnerable man's good triumphs over a vicious man's evil*
> *...slaying the dragon wins the heart of the princess*
> *...perseverance leads to deliverance.*

But as elegant and simple as properly stated themes can be, they still only give us one-half of the stories. Take for example *An Officer and a Gentleman*, the story of Zack Mayo who wants to become a naval officer. One of his physical goals is to successfully complete Officer's Candidate School (OCS) under the harsh tutelage of Gunnery Sergeant Foley. Zack and his bunkmate Sid also have another goal, to have flings with the local blue-collar debs who are hoping to snag officer husbands. Sid pairs up with Lynette, and Zack with Paula. Zack's obstacle of making it through OCS is Sergeant Foley, whose goal it is to get the candidates to drop out, i.e. Drop on Request (DOR). Zack's obstacle in his affair with Paula is that she wants the commitment of marriage, but Zack is unwilling to commit to anyone because his mother and father could never commit to each other or to him. Zack believes that everyone is alone in the world.

Hauge explains the theme of *An Officer and a Gentlemen* like this:

> *In order to be better human beings,*
> *we must give ourselves honestly to others,*
> *but never sacrifice ourselves for others.*[85]

Because the phrase "but never sacrifice ourselves for others" comes from a secondary character's arc (Sid), and because it does not describe the arc of the other main characters (especially Paula), its presence clouds the theme for me. If we eliminate it, we are left with a more focused idea that also (just happens!) to coincide better with one-half of a Moral Premise. Rewording Hauge's theme we have:

> *Giving ourselves honestly to others leads to a better life.*

---

[85] Hauge, pp. 67ff.

But this describes only one-half of the story, albeit the good, the hopeful, the inspirational half. While Zack Mayo, by the end of the movie, does learn that he needs to give himself honestly to his friends (fellow candidates, his love interest, and even his drill sergeant) his decisions during the first half of the movie are based *in values that are opposite the theme*. Because of his parent's dysfunctional values which are exampled in their arrogant and pitiful lives, Zack cannot give himself honestly to others. After his mother checks out by swallowing a bottle of pills, Zack is sent to live with his estranged father in an apartment above a brothel in the Philippines. There Byron Mayo is a U.S. Navy master chief and, evidently, the brothel's chief "whore-master." Zack cannot commit to friends, and consequently his life is the pits.

Thus, the elegance and simplicity of the theme, while helpful as far as it goes, only tells us half of the drama. Although it tells us where the protagonist is going (a wonderful thing for a theme to do), it does not tell us where our protagonist comes from or what obstacles he has to overcome. In other words, the theme does not tell us about the protagonist's physical or psychological conflict. Knowing and seeing the darkness from which the protagonist rises gives a story its power, gives the characters transcendence, and gives us, in the audience, inspiration to live our lives better.

What makes *An Officer and a Gentleman* so powerful is that we are given demonstrations of both halves of the Moral Premise, the good and the bad. At the beginning of the story, Zack thinks only of him-self and uses those around him for his selfish benefit. This gets him in trouble with roommates, his girlfriend, and his drill sergeant. Although Zack is wise enough to recognize and avoid some of the falsehoods around him, he isn't wise enough to see that his selfish arrogance is the very thing that he hates in others. Arrogance, of course, is the belief that we do not need others. Meanwhile, we learn that Sid has put his reliance in his parents' arrogant self interest, and in Lynette, who uses Sid for her own selfish, arrogant interests. Because Sid puts his reliance in these false counselors and friend-ships, his life ends in despair and suicide. Sid's death is like a swift kick in Zack's groin, which is the literal metaphor that Zack sustains at the "hands" of Sergeant Foley. These wake-up calls, which I discuss later as "moments of grace," are the turning points for Zack as he moves along the continuum of the Moral Premise, which can be stated like this:

*Arrogance and dishonesty with others leads to
despair and a life not worth living, but
Giving ourselves honestly to others leads to
hope and a better life.*

Or, more succinctly:

*Deceiving ourselves and others leads to
despair and death; but
Truthfulness to ourselves and others leads to
hope and life.*

Since, the words, "friendship" and "friends" occur frequently in the movie's dialogue, the Moral Premise of *An Officer and a Gentleman* could also be stated:

*Honest friendships and counselors lead to
hope and life; but
Dishonest friendships and counselors lead to
despair and death.*

Let me reinforce that the two phrases of the Moral Premise are exact opposites, and thus describe the decisions and actions of both our protagonist or co-protagonists, reflective or mirror characters, and antagonists or nemeses... all who are necessary to contrast and reveal the power of the drama's message.

In any good drama, this is the power of a correctly stated and thought-out Moral Premise. The Moral Premise shows us the source of our story's conflict, whereas a theme only shows one side. In most successful movies, the protagonist starts off in the bad direction, learns something, and ends up going in the good direction. Likewise, there are friends and associates of the protagonist, some of whom are following the positive side of the Moral Premise, and other characters who are following the negative side of the Moral Premise. In these demonstrative ways the protagonist and the audience are motivated to seek a better life.

Likewise, both parts of the Moral Premise help the writer clearly understand the arc or development of each of the movie's main characters. This gives the entire work a unity of purpose so that it is clearly about one thing. As we will see later, each main character, in a unique way, is challenged by the truth of the Moral Premise and how it impacts their life based on the decisions they make. When they make decisions that are in accordance with the virtue of the Moral Premise, there are good physical and psychological consequences;

In *An Officer and a Gentleman*, Zack hugs Sid's lifeless body as he discovers, like a kick in the groin, the truth of the vice side of the moral premise: *"Deceiving ourselves and others leads to despair and death."* ©2000, Paramount Pictures

and when they make decisions that are in accordance with the vice of the Moral Premise there are bad physical and psychological consequences. The good and bad psychological consequences become the characters' psychological quests, or goals, which also becomes the movie's psychological spine.

Allow me now to take a few pages to explain these relationships, and how the Moral Premise relates to the movie's overall structure.

THE PHYSICAL AND PSYCHOLOGICAL NATURE OF SPINES AND QUESTS

Many terms are used to describe the goals, spines, arcs, quests, and journeys that characters take in motion picture narratives. It's important, before we go on, to clarify how these terms interrelate. There are two categories: physical and psychological.

Table 7 - Physical vs. Psychological Story Descriptors	
Descriptors for Character Goals, Quests, or Journeys, etc.	
Physical Story	Psychological Story
External	Internal
Explicit	Implicit
Outward	Inward
Objective	Emotional
Temporal	Spiritual
Visible	Invisible

Associated with both the physical and psychological aspects of the story is a goal. The protagonist's physical goal is often referred to as the story's quest or the story's spine toward which protagonist and other characters journey. But, there is also a psychological quest or spine... for every outward action began with an inward thought.

The physical quest explains the protagonist's external goal and tells us what the movie is about on the surface. The psychological quest explains the protagonist's internal goal and explains the protagonist's motivation.

The physical quest may be the most important decision in creating a movie. Audiences are *not* first attracted to movies because of themes or Moral Premises; rather it is the physical hook that hauls in the audience. Consider these hooks:

> *Open Water*: Two people alone in an ocean full of sharks seek safety.
> *Finding Nemo*: A single father (in an ocean) seeks his lost son (on land).
> *Schindler's List*: Alcoholic womanizer seeks to save hundreds of Jews from the Holocaust.

But as intriguing as those pitch lines are, the writer of each had to answer untold questions to make those films interesting and meaningful on a psychological level. And that is the job of the psychological quest, or the Moral Premise.

Talking about the inner and outer journeys sounds as if there are really two different stories. But in fact there is *only one story told on two levels*. Even when there are multiple characters and storylines there must be only one psychological or Moral Premise tale. Take for example the wonderfully crafted movie *Love, Actually*, a story with many different physical story lines but only one moral theme — *the purpose of life is to love, actually*. The physical and psychological story elements are totally dependent on each other. As each character seeks what they think is love on a physical level, they discover they are not satisfied until they find love on the psychological level. Only when they accept the psychological aspects of what can be defined as self-sacrificial love of the other, do they find some meaning in the physical realm for themselves.

Likewise, *Die Hard* is about a misplaced New York cop, John McClane, who fights a tower full of murderous thieves, led by the perfect villain, Hans Gruber. The thugs find that McClane is very hard to kill — i.e. he dies hard. But on the psychological level the movie is really about what a man is willing to go through to win back the love of his wife. John's love *dies hard*. In fact, whatever Gruber does, he can't kill John or John's love for Holly. John's trials to defeat the thugs' cavalier disregard for life are metaphors for John's trials to win back Holly's suppressed love.

We cannot see the inner turmoil as John battles his own selfishness and the selfishness of the thugs to get his wife back, but we can see the outward turmoil. We see John and Holly's rejection of each other like we see the rejection of John and the thugs of each other. What the audience identifies in this story, ironically, is *not* what is seen but what is unseen. No one has ever battled thugs in such a circumstance (at least no one I know). Thus, no one can *identify* with that kind of effort. The audience does not identify with how hard it is to battle the hatred of murderous thugs, but many in the audience can identify with how hard it is to battle for the love of an estranged love. The term that irrevocably joins these two stories is *spine* (here implied both physical and psychological). Thus, we can say that the spine of the story is *John's battle with the thugs to save his wife*. In such ways we see time and time again how the physical and psychological stories of successful movies are inexplicably woven together.

Again, let me say that a good way to conceive of movie stories, like *Die Hard* and *Love, Actually*, is to think of the visible story as the metaphor for the invisible story. That is, the psychological goal is revealed by and through the physical goal. Or, the protagonist's inner journey is shown to us in the protagonist's outer journey. This intertwining of inner and outer drama is what makes movies at once both art and mass entertainment. There is nothing else quite like them.

MOMENT OF GRACE: A MOVIE'S FULCRUM OF MEANING

In terms of the Moral Premise, there are some fundamental differences between comedies and tragedies. So, first we need to define what we mean by a comedy or a tragedy. The Greeks classified plays about serious topics (regardless of their outcome) as tragedies, and plays about buffoons and lighter topics as comedies. I think the look on audiences' faces as they walk out of a movie might be a better way to classify what is a classic comedy or what is a classic tragedy. Imagine the classic symbols of drama and comedy, the two masks, one smiling and one frowning. Certainly many "comedies" today are about serious topics, and in some sad-ending movies there are certainly moments of grand levity. So, I think of classic comedies as those movies that leave the audience smiling and feeling good — a movie with a happy ending. While I think of classic tragedies as those movies that leave the audience frowning and feeling bad — a movie with a sad ending.

Therefore, in classic comedies the goals of the protagonist are achieved; whereas in classic tragedies the goals of the protagonist are thwarted. Both types of dramas have psychological and physical spines with related goals, or anti-goals.

Although classic comedies and tragedies are very different kinds of movies, the character arcs of both are shaped by the Moral Premise that give the characters physical and psychological motivation. The Moral Premise does this by reminding the characters of the reward that the virtue offers and the punishment that the vice threatens. This cause and effect, or reward-punishment relationship may not be consciously evident to the protagonist but it must be there, affecting every character in every scene and every line of dialogue. If this consistency is not there, the movie will falter.

COMEDY ARCS

In the spine of a classically constructed comedy (see Figure 1) the protagonist sets off on a physical quest, but because he is unaware of the truth of the Moral Premise, he is thwarted in his progress toward his physical goal. Although the Moral Premise is active throughout the story, there comes a point when the protagonist becomes aware of it and confronts it. This occurs in a scene referred to as the protagonist's "Moment of Grace."

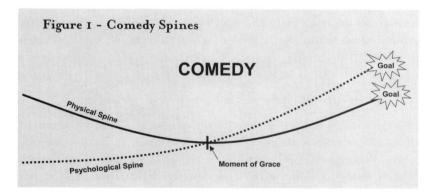

Figure 1 - Comedy Spines

In a classic comedy, the Moment of Grace is that point where the truth of the Moral Premise is offered to a character and accepted. In some films the protagonist sees himself in a mirror (sometimes a real physical mirror, sometimes a symbolic one, and sometimes a moment of self-reflection), recognizes the reality of his situation, and embraces the Moral Premise. From that moment on, his progress toward his physical goal improves, even as he becomes more aware of and applies the Moral Premise's truth. Whereas at the beginning of the story the protagonist is psychologically unaware of the Moral Premise, by the end of the film he realizes that it was the truth of the Moral Premise that was his real goal. Before the Moment of Grace the character makes weak progress along his physical spine. But after the Moment of Grace and the character's acceptance of the truth, the psychological spine lifts and gives strength to the physical spine and to the achievement of the physical goal.

A Beautiful Mind

A Beautiful Mind offers us a great example of how the Moment of Grace involves the protagonist looking into a mirror. The protagonist is John Nash, whose physical quest is to be free from the distractions of his schizophrenic hallucinations so he can concentrate on his work and lead a normal life with his wife. He follows the advice of doctors and bares himself to hospitalization, shock therapy, and drugs. He is unaware of the truth that he needs to discover in order to turn his life around. That truth, in the form of a Moral Premise, could be stated this way:

> *Depending only on others for our well-being leads to impotency; but*
> *Taking responsibility for our well-being leads to productivity.*

The turning point that contains the movie's and John's Moment of Grace comes midway through Act 2 in three dramatic beats — one for Alicia, the co-protagonist, and one for John, the protagonist (both looking into the same mirror), and a third that ties the first two together. The first beat occurs one night in bed as Alicia tries to arouse John sexually. But the medicine, while sedating his hallucinations, has also rendered John impotent. In frustration, Alicia goes into the bathroom, glares at the mirror, sees the bad side of the Moral Premise (John's dependency on her and others), and, in a rage, bangs on the glass mirror, until in a literal way, it symbolically represents their relationship — broken and impotent.

The second beat occurs the next day. John cleans up the shards of the mirror, puts them into a box, and takes them to the trash. Before he discards the broken mirror's shards, he looks into the box and the camera cuts to his POV. For a moment we see what he sees — the face of John Nash reflected in dozens of pieces of broken mirror — a perfect representation of his schizophrenia, and more importantly, a reminder to John that his fate (and his mind, physically seen in the broken mirror's reflection) is in his own hands (as the box is) and not in the hands of others.

The next scene sews the two former beats together as one. It takes place several days later as Alicia brings John his medicine and a glass of water. She turns and leaves before he takes the pill. After she leaves, John opens a desk drawer and discards the pill into a container of other pills. He has stopped taking his medicine. In the days that follow, the hallucinations resurface, but John begins to use a new weapon. His quest for normalcy is the same, but now, embracing the truth of the Moral Premise, we watch the last half of the movie as John takes responsibility for his own health, and through the power of his beautiful mind rejects the hallucinations as such and becomes, again, potent in his work and marriage.

Bruce Almighty

Bruce Almighty offers multiple examples of the Moment of Grace. As discussed later, all main characters can have a Moment of Grace where their progress toward the truth of the Moral Premise shifts. But as is often the case, protagonists are involved in multiple story lines, and each has its own Moment of Grace. Such richness gives the protagonist multiple dimensions, so we can see how the protagonist reacts to the theme of the movie in different circumstances. Examine what happens in *Bruce Almighty*. I will give a brief explanation here, but you might also want to jump ahead to Table 12 — Bruce Nolan's Arc Plots, which shows his four story lines and each Moment of Grace.

Bruce Almighty is about Bruce Nolan, a television news reporter who is particularly gifted at reporting the lighter side of the news. The main physical spine of the movie is Bruce's quest to be the new news anchor. This spine relates to Bruce's career goal. But Bruce has other goals that we'll discover in a moment. Relating to each of the various goals there is but one psychological goal — the psychological spine. It's what the movie is *really* about. In short, Bruce expects miracles to occur to help him reach his goals. Those miracles, he expects, are in the form of others doing the work for him — his boss giving Bruce a promotion without Bruce laboring to earn it, his girlfriend housebreaking the dog without Bruce's participation, or God commanding what Bruce desires. When Bruce doesn't get his way he blames God: "God hates me." When he has to get out of bed to go to work he even puts up a hissie fit. Such is Bruce's level of maturity.

Without going into the entire story, which involves God bestowing his power upon Bruce for a season, Bruce has four physical goals. His *career goal* is to do meaningful work, like becoming the evening news anchor. Bruce's *family goal* is to keep Grace as his girlfriend. A *personal goal* is to housebreak his dog, Sam. And finally, Bruce has a *public goal* to achieve notoriety.

A long form of the Moral Premise for *Bruce Almighty* might be:

> *Expecting miracles, or others to labor with their gifts on our behalf*
> *leads to frustration, anger, and chaos; but*
> *Laboring to be the miracle for others using our gifts for their behalf*
> *leads to contentment, happiness, and peace.*

Now that's kind of long, although it gives us a good picture of the movie. Here's a more succinct rendition.

> *Expecting a miracle leads to frustration; but*
> *Being a miracle leads to peace.*

Along each storyline we see Bruce expecting miracles and not doing much labor to achieve goals using his own naturally occurring gifts or power. He uses other people (and God's power) to achieve his goals. The result is frustration, anger, sadness, and chaos of Armageddon-like proportions. Although there are several moments of grace along this storyline, there is one that is both exactly midway through the movie and also presents Bruce with a problem that he is never able to solve, even with God's power — he begins to hear the prayers of people asking for help. It is at this exact midpoint that Bruce first begins to think of others and not just of himself. It is forced upon him, by virtue of his accepting God's power. Bruce's embrace of the Moral Premise does not happen suddenly, but the turning point occurs here. Out of a 92-minute movie, this Moment of Grace occurs during minute 45.

Bruce Almighty is a significant story also in terms of how the physical story becomes a metaphor for the psychological story. Another way to describe Bruce's journey is by comparing the story of "Grace" (his girlfriend) whom he possesses in a physical sense, with the story of "grace" (his inherent "talents" and power) that he possesses in a psychological sense. As Bruce rejects the naturally occurring *grace* in his life, *Grace* rejects him. It is only when he accepts the *grace* that God has given him, that *Grace* returns. Thus the physical story perfectly metaphors the psychological story.

As in many successful movies, some form of the Moral Premise appears in dialogue, spoken by someone close to the protagonist near the movie's end. In *Bruce Almighty* the crowd surrounding Bruce during his field report about the blood drive speaks the theme of the movie, that is, the positive side of the Moral Premise. It's not a coincidence that the crowd is a curtain call for the movie. All of the characters that interacted with Bruce are present. Throughout the entire movie they have tried to communicate to Bruce the truth of the Moral Premise. Bruce gets it now, and so he lets them say it explicitly for all of them, and to us the audience. At the end of his on-air report, Bruce says, "This is Bruce Nolan down here at the blood drive, reminding you to..." and at that point, Bruce aims his microphone at the crowd behind him who yell, "BE THE MIRACLE!"

TRAGEDY ARCS

Something similar happens in a tragedy but with opposite results. In the spines of classic tragedy (see Figure 2), the protagonist sets off on a physical quest, but because he is unaware of the truth of the Moral Premise he is thwarted in his progress toward his physical goal.

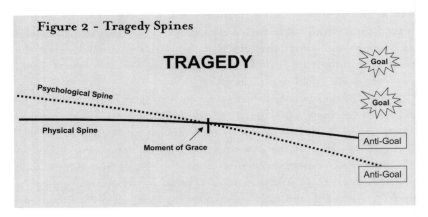

Figure 2 - Tragedy Spines

Although the Moral Premise is active throughout the story, there comes a point when the protagonist becomes aware of it and confronts it in a Moment of Grace. In a tragedy the Moment of Grace is that point when the truth of the Moral Premise is offered to the protagonist but is rejected. From that moment on, his progress toward his physical goal continues to decline, until the ultimate consequence is realized.[86]

In the Bedroom

Most of what I write in this book is about film stories that have happy endings. Those are the most popular and that is why my attention is on them. But let me give one extended example of how a true Moral Premise can be imbued in a very different kind of film, one that not only saw success at the box office (with a budget of only $1.7M, it saw a domestic gross of $36M), but also garnered numerous awards

---

[86] All the main characters in a story should have a Moment of Grace — when they are offered the truth of the Moral Premise and either accept it, reject it, or put it off.

including five Academy Award nominations including Best Adapted Screenplay and Best Picture. I speak of *In the Bedroom*, Todd Field's debut as a director.

In the Bedroom is a story that we might classify as a "family tragedy," which is the "reverse-inverse" (sort of a double negative) of a family romance. In a family romance a man and woman discover ways to: (a) emotionally and physically come together in love, to (b) create a home and give life to children. *In the Bedroom*, by contrast, is about a man and woman who discover ways to: (a) emotionally and physically come apart in hate, to (b) destroy their home and bring death to children.

While the form of the Moral Premise remains the same, *In the Bedroom* takes the negative side to the extreme. Reversing the order of the two halves of the moral premise allows the progression of the negative half, and its extreme, to be seen clearly:

> *[Virtue] leads to [success], and*
> *[Vice] leads to [defeat], but*
> *[Unrelenting vice] leads to [destruction].*

In the Bedroom is based on Andre Dubus' novel *The Killings*. The movie is about how a husband (Dr. Matt Fowler, a family physician) and his wife (Ruth Fowler, a school teacher) refuse to correct their college-bound son Frank's dangerous behavior when he takes up romantically (and sexually) with an older woman (Natalie Strout), who's separated from her jealous and violence-prone husband (Richard Strout). In Act 1 Richard murders Frank in a jealous rage. When the Fowlers seek justice, they discover that Richard Strout has made bail, because of his dad's money and influence as the town's largest employer. In Act 2, the Fowlers also discover that Richard might get off easy by claiming that Frank's death was an accident after they both struggled over a gun. The Fowler's bitterness rages, and in Act 3 they conspire to kill Richard, and eventually carry out the murder with the help of a friend. At the story's end it is obvious to Matt, and to the audience, that their crime was far from perfect. The end of the movie is filled with emptiness, silence, and mind-numbing dread, as both Matt and the audience come to realize that the Fowlers have become what they so hated and imagined in Richard. They will, in all likelihood, be caught, convicted, and punished for the premeditated murder of Richard Strout. Indeed the prognosis for their lives is far worse than the killings of their son, Frank, or of Richard Strout whose deaths came quickly.

Using the two negative lines of the Moral Premise from the previous page, the Moral Premise statement for *In the Bedroom* could be stated this way:

Ignoring moral instruction leads to death and bitterness, but
Flaunting moral instruction leads to killing and dread.

The first half of that statement points to the Fowler's rejection of their Catholic upbringing[87] and a refusal to correct their son's behavior, which leads to Frank's killing and the Fowler's bitterness.[88]

The second half of that statement points to Fowler's further rejection of moral teachings, their conspiracy, their killing of Richard, and the promise of a lifetime of dread and fear of punishment for their crime.

Now, let's look at another slight variation of how this might work. If we take into consideration that Dr. Fowler cares for the physical well-being of the small town and its children, and Ruth Fowler cares for the educational well-being of the town and its children (being caregivers of body and mind as their life goals), another version of

[87] Seven minutes into the film, during a backyard picnic at which Matt and his accomplice Willis tend the barbeque, their priest comes to the picnic. Matt doesn't go to greet him, but shouts across the yard, "Hey, Father! You made it;" to which Fr. McClasslin answers, "Hey, if I don't get to see you fellas here, I don't get to see you at all," indicating that these families are ignoring their past source of moral instruction and discipline.

[88] I was tempted to write a chapter on how the Moral Premise is reflected in character names. That chapter will have to wait. But the name "Frank Fowler" speaks volumes about what *In the Bedroom* is about. Because Frank lacks inhibition (frankness) and because his parents refuse to speak to him likewise with boldness about his indiscretions, the entire family is fouled — having broken the rules they become entangled and offensive to the senses... and they all commit foul deeds. Also, as a verb, "fowl" can mean to "hunt or take wildfowl." A "fowling piece" is a shotgun for shooting wildfowl. In the movie, Frank is the wildfowl who is shot by Richard, who, in turn, is hunted by fowlers.

the Moral Premise could be stated this way:

*Watching over a child's well-being leads to health and life, but
Undermining a child's well-being leads to sickness and death.*

Thus, the first half of that statement refers to the Fowlers' life-time goal of caring for the physical and mental well-being of the town and its children through their medical and educational careers. It is possible that in the backstory, they both professionally cared for Richard Strout, and most definitely for Frank Fowler, their son.

The second half of that statement refers to their undermining Frank's moral well-being, which led to a "moral sickness" and emotional bitterness, in both Richard and the Fowlers, which led both Richard and the Fowlers to kill.

MORE ON THE MOMENT OF GRACE

With that understanding of how the Moral Premise contributes to the dramatic arc, let's look more in depth at the pivotal role of the Moment of Grace. At the beginning of a movie the protagonist is trying to achieve the goal but is either continually thwarted or his progress weakened. Then, at some point, the protagonist turns a corner, albeit a physically subtle one, and begins to make progress. That moment is critical. Something has happened. The protagonist's efforts to achieve the goal take a subtle but decisive turn. The moment is when the Moral Premise plays its most important role of awakening in the mind of the protagonist and the audience what the movie is really about. Psychologically, it's a major turning point.

Later on, I will discuss how we look more specifically at turning points within the Acts, but for right now, let's simplify it.

(1) At the beginning of the movie the main characters behave in one way, but progress toward their physical goal is hindered.

(2) At some point near the middle of the movie (the Moment of Grace) the characters psychologically change the way they behave, although it is often not very noticeable.

(3) After that point, the main characters behave in another way, as progress toward their physical goal changes.

In *A Beautiful Mind*, before the Moment of Grace John Nash tries all kinds of medical treatments to deal with his hallucinations. After the Moment of Grace, John applies the power of his will and reason to marginalize their effect. In *Bruce Almighty*, before the main story's Moment of Grace Bruce Nolan expects miracles to give his life purpose. After the Moment of Grace, Bruce begins to see the need to labor with the graces naturally given to him to give his life purpose. *In the Bedroom's* Moment of Grace occurs when Father McClasslin visits Ruth at her son's gravesite and offers her the opportunity to confess her bitterness — the literal offering of grace through the Sacrament of Reconciliation (Confession). Before that moment, Ruth and Matt suffer internally with the loss. After that moment, they turn their bitterness outward and carry out Richard's murder.

The Moment of Grace is usually triggered by a subtle event that is undergirded by earlier, more dramatic events. It is not the Moment of Grace alone that changes the character's behavior, but it is the "straw that breaks the camel's back."

Liar! Liar!

As another example let's look at *Liar! Liar!*[89] Remember, the Moral Premise must be stated in general enough terms that it applies to millions of people in any place and at any time in history. In simplistic terms, at the beginning of a happy-ending story, our protagonist is behaving badly and practicing some aspect and degree of the vice described in the Moral Premise. But by the end of the movie our protagonist will have learned the truth of the virtue in the Moral Premise and has, to some degree, put that virtue into practice. In *Liar!, Liar!* the Moral Premise might be stated this way:

> *Lying leads to distrust and rejection; but*
> *Telling the truth leads to trustworthiness and admiration.*

At the beginning of the movie Fletcher Reede can't help but lie to everyone around him for the sake of a warped sense of what it takes to be trusted and admired. Fletcher is, in fact, his own antagonist. Fletcher's lying creates a great deal of distrust in him by his son, Max,

---

[89] Yeah, I know, another Shadyac-Carrey movie. But humor me, it illustrates the point clearly on several levels.

and his ex-wife, Audrey. But then Max gets a magical birthday wish —
"For one day, I wish my Dad could only tell the truth." Fletcher is
suddenly and painfully confronted with the truth of his lying ways.
Everything in his life changes, but it's hard to change one's fate in 24
hours. Fletcher is forced to tell the naked and embarrassing truth to
everyone he meets. For a lawyer (rhymes, sort-of, with liar) who
makes his living by lying, Fletcher is in deep trouble. Every time he is
forced to tell the truth, he hates doing it, he tries everything he can
think of to tell a lie, or not to speak the truth. Nothing works. He
can't stand to open his mouth for fear of the consequences.

One of those consequences is that his car is impounded for
dozens of moving and parking infractions. This makes Fletcher late
again for his appointment to play ball with Max. When Fletcher finally shows up, Audrey and Max are sorely disappointed and find it
impossible to trust Fletcher. In a fit of compassion, Audrey bails out
Fletcher's car, and offers up a Moment of Grace to Fletcher by telling
him that she's thinking about moving to Boston to marry Jerry, a
"Magoo" kind of guy who both she and Fletcher know isn't right for
her. It's at this moment that Fletcher sees the error of his ways.
There, in the car pound where Audrey has just offered him physical
grace by getting his car out of hock, Fletcher grabs hold of the psychological grace she offers and for the first time tells her the truth
without remorse. The moment is about halfway through Act 2 (36
minutes 30 seconds in an 80-minute movie). Fletcher seriously and
deliberately tells Audrey: "I'm a bad father. I'm a bad father."

What is startling about his confession is that he says it willingly.
He doesn't fight the truth. He really means it. It is the first time that
he experiences how the truth can truly set him free. Following this,
Fletcher does not suddenly change his ways, but this moment does
begin his long journey toward telling the truth and being reunited
with Max and Audrey. For Fletcher, telling the truth is rewarded with
the trustworthiness and admiration he seeks not only from his family
life, but also in his career.

As a side note, it's interesting to note a very subtle but reinforc-
ing element in the film that reinforces the Moral Premise. Just after
the car pound scene, when Fletcher is told about Max's wish, Fletcher

The Moment of Grace in *Liar! Liar!* Fletcher, without flinching, tells Audrey, "I'm a bad father. I'm a bad father." © 1998, Universal Home Video

rushes to Max's school to get Max to wish again to undo the "truth telling magic." Of course, Max's wish the second time to undo the first wish doesn't work because Max doesn't mean it. But, when Fletcher first comes to the school we hear that Max's teacher is reading to the students Dr. Seuss' *Green Eggs and Ham*. My astute wife Pam points out that *Green Eggs and Ham* is the story of a guy who can't imagine that eating green eggs and ham is any good at all. His friend, Sam, tries all sorts of ways to get his friend to just taste green eggs and ham. Part of the first page goes:

> Do you like green eggs and ham?
> I do not like them, Sam-I-am. I do not like green eggs and
>   ham.
> Would you like them here or there?
> I would not like them here or there. I would not like them
>   anywhere.

That sounds like Fletcher talking about telling the truth. But, when Sam's friend finally gets a taste of green eggs and ham he realizes how good they are. In a similar way, Fletcher is a man that believes that the only thing that could possibly "taste" good in his mouth is a lie. At the Moment of Grace (which occurs just before the *Green Eggs and Ham* scene), Fletcher gets a true taste of telling the truth, and he slowly changes, until at the end of the movie he discovers that he loves the taste of "green eggs and ham."

THE MORAL PREMISE IN MULTIPLE STORY LINES

As already pointed out, the Moral Premise applies to each of the main characters or storylines in your story. After this last section's discussion of *In the Bedroom*, which happens to be a tragic story of dysfunctional parenting, let me shift genres and discuss how the Moral Premise is applied to multiple story lines in the successful television series *7th Heaven*, which happens to be a heroic story of functional parenting.

7th Heaven

In the writer's room at Warner Brothers, *7th Heaven* show-runner and head writer/producer Brenda Hampton is able to consistently apply the principles this book describes. While every *7th Heaven* episode touches on a number of themes, there is always one that is so consistently developed that we can call it a Moral Premise. For instance in "The Fine Art of Parenting" episode, first aired March 14, 2005, the Moral Premise can be stated like this:

> *Proper involvement with your children leads to safety and happiness; but*
> *Not being properly involved with your children*
> *leads to danger and unhappiness.*

The physical stories in this episode feature the conflict between parents being too involved or not involved with their children.

7th Heaven is the continuing story of Rev. Eric and Annie Camden, their seven children, and the many friends, sweethearts and spouses that continually come and go in the Camden household. In this episode, their daughter Lucy and her husband Kevin have a newborn baby, Savannah. While their house is being built, Lucy, Kevin, and Savannah are living with the Camdens. Here the physical conflict results from Annie directly, and Eric indirectly, doing so much for Savannah that Lucy and Kevin are not involved with Savannah as much as they should be. While Lucy is more comfortable around babies, Kevin's opportunities of being involved with Savannah are occupied by everyone else, including dozens of neighbors and friends who stop by to see the baby. This disruption of Lucy and Kevin being involved with their daughter results in conflict between Lucy and Kevin, and indirectly with Annie's help and Eric's hospitality. At the same time, Annie and Eric's involvement with Lucy and Kevin secures their safety and happiness. This particular storyline is, in part, about finding the right degree of involvement in your children's lives.

This takes on another dimension when later on we meet the parents of Vincent, Ruthie's crush. Vincent is struggling for his own identity and a secure relationship with his parents. The root of Vincent's problems are revealed when Rev. Camden talks with Vincent's parents and discovers that when Vincent was just a baby, their family lived with Vincent's grandparents for years, who essentially took care of Vincent and allowed Vincent's parents not to be involved in his life. (The same thing the Camdens are doing with Savannah.) When Vincent's grandparents retired and moved to Hawaii, Vincent's parents suddenly found themselves not knowing how to parent or be normally involved in Vincent's life. Their inability to parent Vincent resulted in unhappiness for the whole family. This sends a signal to Annie not to keep Kevin and Lucy too dependent on her. And it shows Lucy and Kevin that they need to be the primary caregivers for their own child.

Also in this episode is a storyline about Martin, a high school teen who lives in the Camden's garage apartment while his dad serves with the Marines in Iraq. Martin's girlfriend, Zoey, intentionally falls asleep on Martin's couch while they study so she could brag to her friends at school about sleeping with Martin. This raises distrust and sadness with Zoey's parents, Martin, and the Camdens, even when the truth is revealed. The Moral Premise here suggests that had the Camden's been more involved in Martin's life and had Zoey's parents been more involved in her life, Zoey would not have been able to pull off her deception and create such embarrassment.

The final story line involves Eric and Annie's twin boys, Sam and David, who, because Annie is too involved with Lucy and Savannah, make their own lunches to take to kindergarten. This non-involvement results in the boys innocently putting ice cream sandwiches into their brown paper sacks, which melt and make a mess at school.

In each of these very different physical storylines we see explicit examples of how the Moral Premise is applied, e.g. how a parent's proper involvement with their children leads to safety and happiness (for both parents and children), but how, when parents are not properly involved with their children, there is danger and unhappiness.

The Moment of Grace in *A Beautiful Mind*. John Nash sees himself for who he really is, and discovers the secret of his beautiful mind. Just as his mind is capable of looking at the randomness of nature and finding an elegant mathematical solution, so he now confronts his own schizophrenia and finds an elegant solution to his own health. © 2001, Universal Pictures

EXERCISES

1. Contrast and compare the concepts of the *physical story* with the *psychological story*.

2. Contrast and compare the concepts of *theme* and *Moral Premise*, giving comparative examples of each.

3. Study a favorite movie that found box office success, and construct a Moral Premise statement that works for all the main characters. To do this, it will help to discern how the protagonist's method of attaining his or her primary goal differs from the beginning of the movie to the end.

4. In a favorite movie that found box office success, see if you can identify the Moment of Grace. Looking ahead to Chapter 14 may help.

IDENTIFICATION AND THE MORAL PREMISE

6

SUTURING THE AUDIENCE INTO THE STORY

Identification is what draws audience members into the story and allows them to participate with the characters on screen. Identification is not a chance phenomenon. Screenwriters, directors, and editors create identification through decisions of story, script, camera position, staging, art direction, music, and all the other crafts. The filmmaker's purpose is to put audiences into the story and make them a visceral part of the on-screen characters' physical and psychological lives and the story's diegesis (pronounced "die-a-**GEE**-sis").[90] From the standpoint of this book, identification helps audiences to internalize the film's Moral Premise. To pull off identification, filmmakers use a number of techniques collectively called *suturing* (pronounced "**SUE**-chur-ing").

Suturing comes from the idea of sewing pieces of things together to make one bigger thing. To suture (verb) is what a surgeon does to sew pieces of skin or tissue together so your body can heal. A suture (noun) is the seam that unites two separate things. Suturing is what the seamstress does to convert multiple pieces of cloth into a single functional piece of clothing. But in film language, suturing does not refer to splicing separate things together like clips of celluloid film to make a movie, but rather to the process of making individual audience members one with the story. A filmmaker is successful when he connects with his audience on such a level that the audience and the movie are sutured together as one. Suturing is the process of making the ultimate connection. When the audience identifies with the characters in a movie so strongly that the audience's physical and emotional essence is the same as the character's, then there will be strong audience identification with the characters and the story.

---

[90] **Diegesis** refers to the universe of places, ideas, and characters that exists in the imagination that are necessary for the story to work and take place. Its use goes back to Aristotle's *Poetics*.

Just as there are two parts to reality for your audience and characters — the physical and the psychological — so there are two ways that filmmakers can suture an audience into a movie's story. These two ways can be called physical suturing and moral suturing.

PHYSICAL SUTURING

Physical suturing of the audience into the story is done through mechanical means of camera position and editing. The screenwriter, the director, and the editor work together to make the different points of view one point of view, i.e. the filmmakers work to make the audience's point of view the same as the characters' point of view. That point of view, when properly constructed, is not just visual, but aural as well. What the characters see, the audience must see or think they see; and what the characters hear, the audience must hear or think they hear. Of course, intrigue and suspense are part of the storytelling game, and so at times the filmmaker doesn't show the audience what the characters see or hear. But if the process of suturing the audience into the story is done well, the audience will desperately *want* to see and hear what the characters see and hear. The audience will *want* to be *one* with the characters. The audience will want to identify with the characters in every way possible.

A point-of-view (POV) shot is one of the most obvious ways to create physical, visual *suturing*. Another common suturing technique is intercutting between over-the-shoulder shots, or shot/reverse shots that simulate for the audience close approximations of each character's POV. Physical *aural* suturing occurs when filmmakers allow the audience to hear both sides of a telephone conversation — as if the telephone receiver was pressed against the audience's ears.

Another effective physical-visual suturing technique is the long take of an extreme close-up of an actor's face revealing hundreds of minute but larger than life facial muscles as they twinge in sync with the character's thoughts. Physical-aural suturing also occurs when the audience is allowed to hear the protagonist's thoughts, as we do Lester Burnham's in *American Beauty*.

On the psychological level, *Die Hard* is really about what a man is willing to go through to win back the love of his wife. John's love *dies hard*. In the shot before this one, John loosens Gruber's grip on Holly, dropping Gruber to his death, and allowing John to pull Holly up into John's arms. ©1998, Twentieth Century Fox Home Entertainment

Such techniques allow the filmmaker to suture us into the mind and body of the character, and we become an intimate part of the story's diegesis or universe.

Here it is important to note that in addition to the traditional individuals we think of as filmmakers, the exhibitor is also part of the filmmaking process, especially when it comes to suturing audiences into stories. That is because physical suturing is helped tremendously by a theater that is dark and quiet except for the movie's projected image and sound. A dark and quiet theater removes all other physical stimuli of the audience, helping to trick the audience into believing that what they're watching and listening to is not just real, but that they (the audience) are actually there in the story's diegesis.

The most intriguing of the physical suturing techniques that I will describe here is when the filmmaker creates a *gap* in the story-telling. For instance, if in a scene the camera comes to rest exclusively on one of two characters that the audience knows are in a room, and totally excludes from view the second character... then after a while the audience fills in the physical visual gap. That is, either the audience imagines the second character, or, better still, if the camera angles are close to the second character's POV, the audience will fill the visual gap by putting themselves into the place of the other character.

Another technique of creating physical gaps in the story that the audience fills in, is to compress the story time by eliminating visuals and sounds associated with nonessential story elements. For instance, when a character moves from location A to location B across a city, the filmmaker may only *suggest* the means of conveyance, the time of day, the difficulty of the trip, the weather, and so on. Each audience member will automatically fill in the gap with their own experiences of traveling across town in a cab, during rush hour, in a rainstorm. Thus, audience members become physically and intimately sutured into the life of the character.

Use of these mechanical suturing techniques, which practically force audiences to identify with the story's physical nature, is the first step in connecting the audience to the story's universe. But the second step is even more important. Just as physical suturing draws the audience into the physical premise of the story, so moral suturing draws the audience into the Moral Premise.

MORAL SUTURING

Moral premises in movies only work when they resonate with audiences as true. The truth or falsehood of a movie's Moral Premise is not something audiences consciously recognize, at least not typically. At the end of *Die Hard* we're consciously thinking about how John McClane defeated the bad guys, but subconsciously we are probably aware that the movie was about how a man's love for his wife dies hard. The love that John has for Holly, along with his hatred of evil, was at the center of his motivation and gave the movie its psychological drive. Such resonance occurs due to implicit or even symptomatic elements.[91] If the Moral Premise is consistently portrayed throughout the movie, and if it's true to the natural order of things with which the audience is acquainted, then audience members will be sutured into the movie on a psychological level. Audiences will identify with the movie's diegesis and recognize its rules as true. They will find

---

[91] There's a difference between implicit, which means the filmmaker made a conscious effort to include the element, and symptomatic, which means the filmmaker did something subconsciously to include the element.

themselves subliminally agreeing with the moral and psychological story that the filmmakers have created. That agreement is part of why you tell others about a film you like. You have identified with the characters' moral struggle, you have rooted for them, and just as if the movie was an emotional journey in your own life, you will be anxious to tell others about it and recommend they see it, too.

Michael Hauge makes this same point in his discussion of *An Officer and a Gentleman*. People didn't come out of that movie consciously aware of the movie's theme by "declaring, 'I loved that movie! I, too, believe we must give ourselves to others, but never sacrifice ourselves.' That would be absurd. If anything, they were saying, 'Richard Gere! Hey, what a hunk!'" Yet, at the same time, Hauge points to something that is absolutely true. The theme reaches the audience on a "much deeper, more subtle level than that of the plot... a level of understanding that is subconscious but still very real"[92] and one that connects with the audience's values and gives their own life, complete with trials and conflicts, great meaning. That level of identification gives audiences a deep, although non-verbalized, satisfaction that they pass on to their friends with word-of-mouth recommendations.

On the other hand, if the Moral Premise is inconsistently portrayed, or if the Moral Premise is not true to the natural order with which the audience is acquainted, then audience members will not be sutured into the movie on a psychological level. What if John McClane looked for a way out of the tower at all costs and refused to sacrifice his well-being for his wife? What if he were to have shown ambivalence toward what the thugs were doing? What if *Die Hard* were about John protecting his own life and even showed him willing to sacrifice Holly to protect himself? In that case the Moral Premise might have been:

> *"Covetous hatred leads to life and celebration, but Sacrificial love leads to self-denial and certain death."*

In such a case my guess is that audiences would not identify with the movie's diegesis and they would not recognize its rules as true. That

---

[92] Hauge, p. 79.

is, they would have found themselves subliminally disagreeing with the moral and psychological space that the filmmakers created. The movie would have bombed at the box office, if it had gotten made at all. Such lack of identification greatly decreases an audience's likelihood of recommending the movie to their friends.

IDENTIFICATION PATTERNS

The more we look at successful and not-so-successful movies through the lens of a Moral Premise we discover that when Moral Premises are true and consistently applied throughout the movie it has a much better chance at success than if the Moral Premises applied are falsely or inconsistently applied. When we look at a large number of films and compare the truth of the Moral Premise with its box office success, patterns beyond simple box office numbers emerge.

1. Audiences recognize that natural law contains a system of moral absolutes.

In successful movies, characters react to moral absolutes regardless of the laws of man or their own selfish desires. In fact, in many successful movies the protagonist obeys a moral absolute that operates outside the legal order of the diegesis and beyond the protagonist's own selfish desires. James Bond thinks nothing of breaking his country's rules if there is a higher moral absolute that he (and the audience) believes must be obeyed; and his own selfish interests are not considered until the last scene when, "Oh, by the way... " he gets the girl.

Detroit Detective Axel Foley (*Beverly Hills Cop*) disobeys his superior's instructions and numerous state laws to catch his bad guys. Foley believes that if he followed man-made rules he would jeopardize the moral absolute of justice.

Matt and Ruth Fowler (*In The Bedroom*) take man's and nature's laws into their own hands and avenge the killing of their son; but before they are even suspected of the crime, they pay the price of answering to a moral absolute that says killing and revenge are wrong.

Ted Stroehmann's love for Mary Jensen (*There's Something About Mary*) gets nowhere until Ted realizes that love is not about satisfying his own selfish desires, but rather about an absolute rule that demands he sacrifice his desires for the good and happiness of Mary.

2. Moral choices have consequences consistent with natural law.

Even though moral choices can sometimes be great dilemmas, when a character follows the natural moral order of things (revealing a virtue) the character should reap some level of happiness and satisfaction. Bond gets his man... and girl. Foley solves the crime... and all is forgiven. When characters choose to reject natural moral order (revealing a vice), they should reap some level of unhappiness and find little or no satisfaction. Even before the police are aware that a murder has been committed, the Fowlers are caught in their own trap and entombed with mind-numbing guilt and fear. Ted's selfish pursuit of Mary results in one wacky problem for Ted after another, but when he follows the natural law of selflessness, the results are much more satisfying.

3. Suffering, which is a consequence of natural law, can lead to purpose and hope.

Characters who look for meaning in their suffering and react to it in accordance with a true Moral Premise will find purpose and hope for their lives. For example, James Bond, Alex Foley, and John McClane all suffer physical and psychological trauma, but in the end, when their foes are vanquished, they and the audience experience deep satisfaction and hope for the future. And, Ted Stroehmann's sufferings teach him that thinking of others first is much more satisfying than thinking only of himself, if for no other reason than that he gets Mary's respect. But characters who reject the idea that suffering is a meaningful part of natural law will find little or no purpose or hope for their lives. The Fowlers, for instance, reject the consequences of natural law and man's law, flaunt both, and face a future of dread.

Research[93] involving similar movies reveals that when characters choose what seems naturally *right* and reap in the end what seems

---

[93] The conclusions drawn in this paragraph and elsewhere in this book are based on formal and informal research conducted by the author discussed in the Appendix. The conclusions assume that the motion pictures being compared are similar in production value, with a good director, accomplished actors, and skilled cinematography. When comparing box office success there must have been a serious effort on the part of the distributor to establish the movies' trade names with national advertising and a reasonable, not limited, number of prints.

naturally *good*, audiences recognize the moral truth of that story and reward it with a strong showing at the box office. When characters choose what seems naturally *wrong* and reap in the end what seems naturally *good*, audiences recognize the moral falsehood of the story and the box office numbers fail to live up to expectations. In the former, audiences identify with the story and characters on a sympathetic and emotional level rooted in the audience's perception of moral absolutes. In the latter, audiences do not identify with the story or its characters; there is little or no sympathy or emotional connection because the audience perceives the story to be morally false.

A good example of this is Nicolas Cage's vehicle *Gone in 60 Seconds*. As fun as it is to see if Randall 'Memphis' Raines, a retired master car thief, and his team can steal 50 hot cars in one night in order to save Raines' brother's life, the audience probably feels uneasy with the idea that grand theft auto on such a scale could be justified to save a screwed-up, undeserving brother. But under Raines' willingness to do the deed are the moral virtues of grace, mercy, and sacrificial love that recruits audience members as willing accomplices. We can taste the palatable double dilemma Raines faces throughout the night of heists. We wonder how he can pull off such a lush caper: He must not only pull off an unprecedented number of grand thefts, but he cannot be caught and sent back to prison, he must rescue his brother, and finally he must keep himself from getting killed by the antagonist. The uncomfortable feeling the audience experiences during most of the movie is the result of our identification with Raines' character — we're glad we're not in his shoes. We're glad we rarely have to face such a moral paradox. We never want to step into a situation that is clearly morally wrong with only the slightest prospect of bringing about a higher moral good. But we hope Raines can do it because we know his motivation embraces those natural moral truths that value life more than 50 high-priced cars. Fortunately, the filmmakers knew what they were doing and never lost sight of the moral justification of what Raines is doing or what he has planned, unbeknownst to the audience and stolen-car broker. If you haven't seen the movie I'll not spoil the sting ending. Suffice it to say, Raines' actions, although at first they appear morally wrong, are in fact an elaborate ploy at reinstating justice and the natural order. We applauded him for it... and rewarded the producers with word-of-mouth promotion.

Just as gravity and its consequences are part of our physical universe, so the acknowledgement of moral absolutes, moral consequences, and the purpose of suffering are likewise written into our own personal psychological reality. When filmmakers acknowledge such truths and incorporate them into their stories, they naturally suture their audience into the story's fabric with satisfying results at the box office.

AUDIENCE/FILMMAKER VALUE ALIGNMENT

Here is a graphic way to explain what I discussed a few paragraphs back. When an audience identifies with the characters in a movie, a connection is made between the audience and the filmmaker... and the filmmaker's message and its meaning are easily passed on to the audience. But if audiences cannot identify with the characters then there is a disconnect between the filmmaker and his audience... and the filmmaker's message is either lost or misconstrued. Why, at times, might an audience not be able to "fill the gaps" or "identify with the film" and "see" its meaning? One reason is because the psychological realities of the filmmaker and his audience are not aligned.

This alignment begins with the screenwriter or director, of course, when the story first takes form, and the Moral Premise is constructed, whether consciously or unconsciously. Dana Cooper has this advice for writers.

> There's also an important issue of integrity regarding the dramatic equation [Moral Premise]... the implied statement of your story [must be] essentially true. Even if it's just a comic romp, there is a statement of relative values in every screenplay. Beware that if you don't believe the logic, world-view, and values expressed in the outcome message, your internal doubt will cause repeated problems, including creative resistance and even "shutdown."[94]

---

[94] Cooper, p. 77.

Audience identification and the alignment of moral reality between the audience and filmmaker have a joint effect on a film's popularity. Figures 3 and 4 illustrate the two extreme modes of the identification process between an audience and a filmmaker and will help to illustrate this phenomenon.

Figure 3 - Nonaligned Moral Realities: Invalid Audience Identification

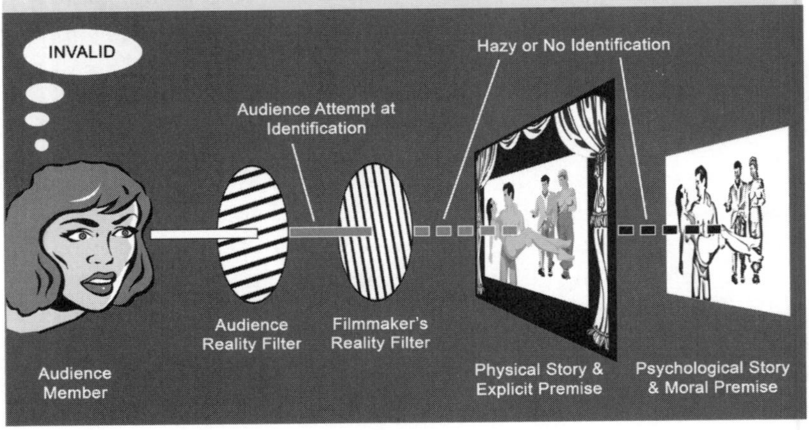

In Figure 3, polarized filters set 90 degrees to each other represent the audience's different perception of moral reality with that of the film-maker's. As the audience member looks through the filters at the movie, her identification with the film's physical story and psychological story (and the respective premises) is blocked or at best made hazy. The audience member "just does not get it" and leaves with the subconscious perception that the film is "invalid." The audience member says to her friends, "I didn't like it," and the word-of-mouth recommendation will likely be negative.

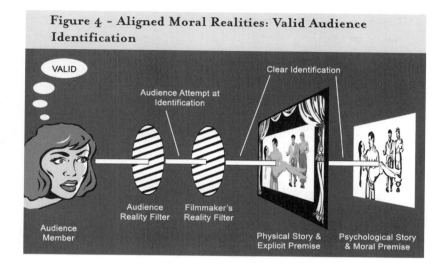

Figure 4 - Aligned Moral Realities: Valid Audience Identification

In Figure 4, the filmmaker's and the audience member's moral reality filters are aligned, allowing the audience member to establish clear sympathetic identification with the film; the resulting subconscious perception is that the film is "valid." The audience member says to her friends, "I liked it," and the word-of-mouth recommendation will likely be positive.

Note that we are not discussing the explicit or physical story line but the psychological or Moral Premise storyline. The models illustrated in Figures 3 and 4 depict whether or not the audience is sutured into the movie's moral meaning and thus their ability to understand what the movie is *really* about.

WHAT THE MOVIE IS *REALLY* ABOUT

As we get close to the Strategic Processes and the Tactical Steps of Part II, it's important that we understand the difference between what a movie is about and what it is *really* about. Yes, I've mentioned this several times before, but the structure of the film's story arcs are critically related to this concept. So, let me summarize these last few chapters on theory and then answer a few of my critics before we get to Part II.

Remember, although movies are said to be generally *about* things that can be seen — that is things in the *physical* realm — popular movies are *really about* things in the *psychological* realm that cannot be seen. That is why we talk about what a movie is "about," and then talk about what the movie is "*really* about."

When a writer knows his movie's Moral Premise, he knows the reasons for his story and the true psychological motivations of his characters. That knowledge is the basis for making every structural decision about the story, including the characters' arcs, the plot's turning points, the setting's characteristics, and even scenes and dialogue structure. The Moral Premise also provides direction to each of the actors, the director of photography, the production designer, the art director, and the distributor's marketing director. The key for each of these people is to know the story's central idea, its implicit message, its emotional arc… its *Moral Premise*.

Now, my critics will claim that a movie does not have to have a theme, a message, or a Moral Premise to be successful. To bring evidence to their argument they point to "pure" action fare such as the James Bond films or Schwarzenegger vehicles like *The Terminator* series. But to me such films are ripe with themes, messages, and Moral Premises.

Although the Bond character may not journey through a redemptive arc, the movies still communicate a clear theme that could be stated this way:

> *The pursuit of power leads to death and defeat; while*
> *The pursuit of justice leads to life and success.*

In terms of political messages, one might interpret the Bond films as idealizing the role of government espionage, secrecy, and the secret agent of a Western government who has "a license to kill" and can act with impunity. A log line that includes a parliamentary inquiry into the legalities of Agent 007's actions is not an acceptable pitch for a Bond flick (unless the inquiring member of parliament is the antagonist's mole). Now, admittedly, we don't take all of this as serious political propaganda, it all seems like such harmless fun. But the themes and political messages are still clearly evident.

When it comes to films like Schwarzenegger's *Terminator* movies, the moral and spiritual themes are as vivid as some of the special effects. For instance, in *Terminator 2*, the Terminator returns to the present day to save Sarah and John from being terminated by the new T-2000 cyborg. After the Terminator destroys the T-2000, he prepares to lower himself into a boiling cauldron of molten metal. Sarah pleads with him to stop.

SARAH
It's over.

TERMINATOR
No. There's one more chip...

The Terminator points to his head.

TERMINATOR
...and it must be destroyed also.

At the Terminator's request and against John's protest, Sarah lowers the Terminator into the fiery pit where "he" and the chip are destroyed. Throughout the film this Moral Premise is made exceedingly clear:

> *Sacrificial love leads to life; but*
> *Hatred leads to death.*

The same is true of the best of the other action films such as the *Die Hard* and *Lethal Weapon* series. Here not only does good triumph over evil, but the value and importance of the traditional family is reinforced by the protagonists either trying to put their families back together, or saving them from certain destruction. More on this later.

Before we go on, let me put one more nail in the coffin that movies don't need to have a message or deeper meaning to be successful. For this let me call Robert McKee to the witness stand. In *Story* he writes:

STORYTELLING is the creative demonstration of truth. A story is the living proof of an idea, the conversion of idea to

action. A story's event structure is the means by which you first express, then prove your idea... without explanation.[95]

In that short paragraph McKee uses the term "idea" three times to define the earlier term "truth." Yeah, McKee gets philosophical on us. What he's trying to tell us is that storytelling is basically a philosophical pursuit wherein we explore what is true and false, and how to live our lives better and happier. He uses the word "proof" here in a philosophical and logical sense. He's saying that stories don't try to prove the reality of the explicit plot (e.g. cyborgs exist and can return to the present day), but that stories communicate and teach an idea that is philosophically true — true love willingly sacrifices for the good of the other.

And that is what movies are *really* about.

By now, if I've done my job, you may be beginning to believe that to write and make a great movie you really need to imbue it with a true Moral Premise.

But how?

Good question.

That's why I wrote Part II.

---

[95] McKee, p. 113. Capitalization and bold are McKee's.

EXERCISES

1. List and briefly explain the different ways a filmmaker *physically* helps the audience identify with the film's characters.

2. List and briefly explain the different ways a filmmaker *morally* helps the audience identify with the film's characters.

3. Study a successful movie and describe several specific ways the film-maker physically and morally sutured the audience into the story.

4. From a number of the top box office films you've recently seen, write out the physical premise for the story (what the movie is about), and contrast that with the psychological story of the movie (what the movie is *really* about). Then describe the metaphor that relates them.

II

Application

PART

*The chapters in this part describe
an Eight-Step process for incorporating a true Moral Premise
into a film story's structure.*

*The eight chapters that describe
the steps (8-13 and 15-16) are
very short. Chapters 7, 14, and
17, however, provide additional
support about strategic planning,
arc plot tables, and a final capstone example. Altogether, these
chapters explain the nitty-gritty
of fleshing out the Moral
Premise, creating character arcs,
and, finally, sequencing the
major dramatic beats to a story
that will make the writing of your
story treatment and first draft of
your screenplay smooth sailing.*

I promise: No writer's block!

STRATEGIC PROCESSES

7

BEGIN WITH THE END IN MIND

Stephen Covey in *Seven Habits of Highly Effective People* writes: "Begin with the End in Mind."[96] Know where you're going before you start the car and pull out of the garage. File a flight plan before taxiing to the runway. Beginning with what you want to end up with is consistent with good planning. Before a building is constructed the owners describe to the architect the building's purpose and end use; and that end use drives every structural decision from where the entrance-exits are to be placed, to the type of furniture, the mechanical equipment that needs to be installed, and even the decor. Beginning with the end in mind is what we do when we take a trip — we first ask ourselves where we want to go and how quick... and then we plan the precise route and stops, or lack of them, along the way.

This makes sense when writing a screenplay or directing a movie. When we write a screenplay, knowing what the story is *really* about and thus how it ends, can drive the structure of the story's plot and mold decisions about the character's physical and moral journeys to their logical and satisfying end.

The Moral Premise statement describes the psychological *end* of the story, depending on whether a character accepts the vice or the virtue. Because we've also described the physical goal for the protagonist, the physical end is simple to figure out. If the protagonist follows the vice, he fails to achieve his desired physical end and experiences its opposite. If the protagonist follows the virtue, he is tempted with the vice, but in the end he achieves his desired physical goal.

If you're going to construct a successful screenplay, you have to start with these endings. It really does not matter which, physical or psychological. But once you establish your protagonist's physical quest, or what your movie is about in the physical realm, you will make

---

[96] Covey, pp. 95 ff.

your job measurably easier if you take time to develop your protagonist's psychological quest, or what your movie is really about. Because once you do so, you'll be starting with the end in mind. The sooner your Moral Premise is articulated, the more efficient you will become in making all the other ancillary creative decisions so that the storylines all come together, in the end, at the same point.

Beginning with the end in mind allows you to construct the structure of a screenplay story with fewer steps. It follows that you will use less energy, less time, and be more effective. As W. Edwards Deming, father of Statistical Process Control, was fond of saying: "It costs just as much to make a bad part as it does a good one. So, why not make a good one in the first place."[97] Why not structure a screenplay the right way the first time and eliminate some of that re-writing cost and energy?

HARE BRAIN, TORTOISE MIND

Some accuse me of being too linear, or left-brained, as if true artists were only supposed to use the right half of their grey matter. In truth, I believe you need both halves of your noggin to be a successful writer. There's a great book that Writer/Director Ed Solomon recommended to me titled *Hare Brain, Tortoise Mind: How Intelligence Increases When You Think Less* by Guy Claxton (a British psychologist with Zen Buddhist leanings). The book represents a good balance to the predominantly left-brained process that I outline in Part II. Claxton reminds us of the importance of assimilation and non-linear thinking. He derides linearity (or what he calls "d-mode" thinking) in favor of the unconscious or "undermine."[98] People who meditate will identify quickly with what Claxton says. Meditation is the sinew, if you will, that helps tie the left-brain process steps that follow together. When I meditate, pull weeds, drive somewhere, or any other activity that relaxes my mind, ideas flow out of the subconscious that solve problems my left-brain can't by itself. Yes, what follows is decidedly left-brain. But before you start you will also need to access your right brain by planning regular sessions of relaxation and meditation. You have to use

---

[97] Deming said this in countless interviews, even one with the author in a documentary for Ford Motor Company in 1981.

[98] Claxton, p. 34, ff.

your left and right brains together. As I've said before, filmmaking is a collaboration... of minds.

So much for the strategic stuff. Let's mind our work.

TACTICAL STEPS

Eight of the next ten chapters are very short — they are steps you can use to structure a screenplay around a true Moral Premise. I readily admit that there are countless permutations of these steps that will also work. What is important is not the exact order of each step, but each step's end purpose. In fact, I'll go so far as to say that following the steps is not important at all, as long as the end result is achieved. In such a case, the steps function merely as an outline of how the story, in the end, should interrelate with respect to the Moral Premise. Remember what we covered back in Chapter 4 about the different ways artists can engage and succeed in the storytelling art. For the sake of expediency, however, let me explain these steps with my thinking cap tilted to the left.

To a great extent the process must be cyclical and iterative, which means that the process will benefit by repeating certain steps to take into account the decisions made later on. All the decisions and elements of your story must end up as a harmonious whole. And the various decisions are co-dependent on each other. For instance, a decision in Step 4 may cause you to rethink decisions made in Step 2, which in turn will likely effect Step 3 and 4 decisions. As you go through this iterative process, the scope and impact of the decisions becomes less and less, and the whole takes on a well-integrated, gestalt life of its own.

You are different from other readers of this book, and each story you write will take a slightly different path based on a host of parameters including your familiarity with the topic, life experiences, research, location scouting, what you had for breakfast, whether or not you have a date for the weekend, and the coverage you get from others. But for now, let me try to explain the process in numerical order. It will be easier for me, and hopefully easier for you to follow.

Here we go.

STEP 1.
DETERMINE THE CONTROLLING VIRTUE

8

THE STORY'S VIRTUOUS THEME

A controlling virtue, of course, is a value that you, the writer, must hold in the highest esteem. It is something you are passionate about getting more of; something that gets you out of bed in the morning to write about. It has to be a value that connects with your view of humanity on every level. It is something that is eternally true, and hopefully of importance to most, if not every member of society... your audience. For instance, I'm revising this section a day after Ashley Smith, single mom, was taken hostage by Brian Nichols, who escaped from an Atlanta Courtroom by over-powering a guard, taking the guard's gun, and killing four people in the process. Ashley, tied up in her apartment, won Brian's trust by showing him respect and demonstrating compassion for his ordeal, even cooking pancakes for his breakfast with "real butter." The result? He releases her, she calls 911, and Brian gives up without a fight. He didn't want to hurt anyone else. The controlling virtue of this story could be narrowed down as "compassion" and the story's theme stated as "compassion leads to understanding and peace." That is a controlling virtue.

Hundreds of movies have been made about virtues such as friendship, loyalty, fidelity, honor, courage, sacrifice, love, perseverance, generosity, humility, honesty, kindness, justice, patience, cleverness, unity, and freedom. We can keep making movies about these same virtues because a true virtue reveals itself in a 1001 ways.[99] Virtues are things we all strive for but never fully achieve. And so we keep coming back to them hoping to acquire a bit more of the virtue's substance to make our life, and the lives of others, a little better.

When you've selected a controlling virtue, move on to Step 2.

---

[99] The controlling virtue embedded in a story must be true for it to be accepted by the public. For instance, if a story is constructed that generally values anarchy as a moral good, audiences will see the story as endorsing a false virtue and stay away.

STEP 2.
DETERMINE THE CONTROLLING VICE

9

THE VIRTUE'S ANTAGONIST

One of the reasons we never achieve our full measure of virtues is because of the vices that oppose our best efforts. Vices are those things that you, the writer, loathe. They are things that you are passionate about eliminating from reality, if you could. Vices get you out of bed in the morning through fear and anger. But just as often, vices are passive-aggressive in nature — they prevent accomplishment through inaction, disinterest, apathy, paranoia, polemics, and ambivalence.

Depending on your mindset and personal motivation, it may be that you choose a controlling vice for your movie before you choose a controlling virtue. Successful movies, of course, must have a great antagonist whose vices would motivate the laziest person to action. The brashness of the villain must rival, if not be greater than, the courage of the hero. In *Die Hard*, John McClane would be easily forgotten if it wasn't for the villainous Hans Gruber. So starting with a controlling vice can be very productive.

Now, as you might expect, the controlling vice and controlling virtue must be opposite each other. So that you can see this better, I've paired the virtues of Step 1 with their opposites in Table 8.

Table 8 - Virtue-Vice Pairs

Virtues	Vices
Friendship	Betrayal
Loyalty	Abandonment
Fidelity	Unfaithfulness
Honor	Dishonor
Courage	Desertion
Sacrifice	Selfishness
Love	Hatred
Perseverance	Slothfulness
Generosity	Greed
Humility	Pride
Honesty	Hypocrisy
Kindness	Cruelty
Justice	Injustice
Patience	Impatience
Cleverness	Rashness
Unity	Division
Freedom	Imprisonment

Once you select the motivating vices and opposing virtues, you are ready to give your characters depth. That means, of course, assigning vices to your hero, and virtues to your villain. Yes, I wrote that correctly... *vices* to your *hero* and *virtues* to your *villain*. This gives your characters depth. The villain's virtues often provide some sympathy for their characters and may even explain why, in their misguided way, they do what they do. For instance, Hans Gruber in *Die Hard* saw himself as a modern-day Robin Hood. At the same time, giving your hero vices provides not only humanistic qualities (no one is perfect) but also gives the hero a fault to work on that can improve by the story's end, or a quirk that seems to improve but ultimately reverts. For instance, in *Die Hard*, John McClane's pride also dies hard, but Hans Gruber humbles John and makes him a better companion for Holly.

Ah-ha! Now that there's evil afoot to challenge the virtue, we have a chance at a successful movie. Go to step 3.

STEP 3.
DETERMINE THE MORAL PREMISE

10

THE STORY'S ULTIMATE MESSAGE

What the movie is *really* about is the message or *Moral Premise statement*. Write out a rough approximation of your movie's Moral Premise. I say rough, because as the process continues, and your story develops, you'll come back to this step time and time again to refine the wording. At least for now, get something written down. It will help you focus. Use whichever format helps you best:

> *[Vice] leads to [undesirable consequences], but*
> *[Virtue] leads to [desirable consequences];*

or

> *[Vice] leads to [defeat]; but*
> *[virtue] leads to [success].*

It may be helpful to think of the *defeat* and *success* as the *physical* goals, and *vice* and *virtue* as the *psychological* goals of the same characters. Here are several simple examples:

> > *Foolishness leads to death; but wisdom leads to life.*
> > *Bragging leads to humiliation; but humility leads to honor.*
> > *Selfishness leads to isolation; but selflessness leads to community.*
> > *Unbridled passion leads to risk; reasoned discernment leads to safety.*

Finally, the Moral Premise statement must be a natural law, an absolute truth. It must be true for any person, anywhere, throughout time. Thus, it must be general. Your story is very specific, but this truth, upon which your story is based, is the identifying element for your audience of millions. If you want to write a movie for anarchists and their "friends," ignore this advice. Otherwise, memorize your moral premise and advance to Step 4.

11

STEP 4.
DETERMINE THE MOVIE'S GENRE

THE ARC OF CULTURAL CONFLICT AND RESOLUTION

Genre films create certain audience expectations for the protagonist. Often the protagonist's arc is known by the audience before the movie begins. Such expectations about the construction of genres may predetermine how the protagonist reacts to the story's moral premise and conflict. This is because, as Thomas Schatz explains in *Hollywood Genres*, genre movies deal with fundamental cultural conflicts that can never be ultimately resolved but yet offer a solution, if only temporary and idealistic. Schatz refers to these fundamental, never-truly-to-be-resolved conflicts as the "static nucleus" of genre stories, and the resolution as the film's "dynamic surface structure."[100]

In these terms, Westerns are stories about rugged individualism; that is, a hero who helps a community resolve a problem of social integration that brings about a new social order. But in the end, our Western hero returns to his individual ways and cannot himself be integrated into the new order.

In the Gangster flick, the hero is perverted by social forces of unemployment or injustice. And yet the movie's resolution comes about through the gangster's death at the hands of that social order in an effort to conquer anarchy, while simultaneously celebrating the gangster's loyalty to family.

In the Romantic Comedy the fundamental differences between the sexes are temporarily resolved through a new order of compromise for the sake of love. But after the wedding, everyone expects the sparks to fly again.

Genre, therefore, helps define and describe the arc that the story, and thus each character, is expected to take as they test and then embrace or reject the Moral Premise. While I do not advocate a formalistic embrace of classic genre patterns, and I do not believe that a

---

[100] Schatz, p. 31.

particular Moral Premise demands a specific genre, the choosing of a genre does set audience expectations, if only to surprise them.

This allows creative license to choose a true moral premise that may appear on the surface to be contradictory to the genre's expected outcome. That is, by choosing a Moral Premise that twists the expectation of a genre, you may discover an entirely new and fresh combination that will delight audiences. Spend time contemplating such a combination until you can see and feel the flow of the story. Don't worry at first about working out the details, although eventually you'll need to defend the protagonist's journey as whole and satisfying, even if ironic.

A great example of this is Jon Springer's popular zombie short *Living Dead Girl*. The zombie subgenre was revolutionized and universally defined by filmmaker George A. Romero in his 1968 horror masterpiece, *Night of the Living Dead*. The zombie subgenre now demands that: 1) Zombies seek out and feed on living flesh; and 2) when a zombie takes a bite out of a normal, living person, that person dies, and subsequently rises again to become yet another member of the walking dead — a zombie destined to likewise seek out human flesh. But Springer took a Moral Premise from an unlikely source — Catholicism — twisting the subgenre results with surprising popularity. Catholics believe that when the communion bread and wine are brought to the altar and offered by the priest in the name of Christ in the Eucharistic sacrifice, they become the literal body and blood of Jesus Christ. This sacramental bread and wine are then distributed to the congregation who "literally" eat and drink the body of Christ.[101] The Moral Premise embedded in every Mass can be stated like this:

Not eating the body of Christ leads to death; but
Eating the body of Christ leads to life.

So, theorized Springer, what happens when a zombie encounters Jesus Christ, in the living flesh standing on a street corner? In *Living Dead Girl*, when the zombie takes a bite out of Christ's arm, rather than Christ turning into a zombie as the genre suggests, the zombie instead

---

[101] Non-Catholics may find this odd, but Catholics point to the Gospel of John, Chapter 6, that provides story and teaching, along with centuries-old rituals from the Mass.

comes back to life, an unexpected plot twist but one that resonates with truth among those familiar with the Catholic Mass. The juxtaposition of this Moral Premise and a well-known subgenre gives an entirely new and fresh perspective to a short that has received wide praise — indeed rave reviews — on many popular independent film websites, such as *Film Threat* and *Ain't It Cool News*.

So, look for interesting and surprising ways to combine Moral Premises and genres. You may hit on something no one else has thought of.

Now, by combining Moral Premise and genre expectations you should know and be able to articulate the moral and generic structure of your story. Congratulations! This is a significant accomplishment. You're ready for Step 5.

STEP 5. DETERMINE THE PROTAGONIST'S PHYSICAL GOAL

12

THE MOVIE'S PHYSICAL SPINE

Although you may have done this earlier, write down the protagonist's external or physical goal. This is the same thing as the movie's physical spine, or what the movie is "about." For example: Frodo must resist the Ring's evil power and cast it into the fires of Mount Doom, or Randall Raines must steal 50 cars in one night and rescue his brother.

Since you know what the movie is really about from Step 3, this step describes the metaphor of that truth in a demonstrative, physical way. When Step 3 and Step 5 are appropriately related, the chances of writer's block are dramatically reduced, if not rendered impossible.

You may have started structuring your story at this step. That is, the physical arc of the story and the protagonist's goal may have come to your mind first. This may have occurred after being intrigued by a news story, listening to tales around the dinner table, or knocking about a "what if" scenario with friends. Discovering such "hooks" is often the way some of the best movies get started.

If you do begin at this step, with the physical spine, I strongly suggest that you go back and figure out Steps 1-4, then revisit this step (Step 5), before you continue to Step 6. You'll save yourself a lot of time.

STEP 6. DETERMINE THE PROTAGONIST'S PHYSICAL OBSTACLES

THE MOVIE'S PHYSICAL CONFLICT

This step is about the same level of difficulty as Step 5 and may come to you at the same time. Identifying the obstacles that prevent the protagonist from achieving his or her physical goal may occur to you before the goal is clear. Just remember, something is only an obstacle because there is a goal in the first place. So make sure you know clearly what the physical goal is and make sure your protagonist knows it.

As you make this journey of discovery, your protagonist may have a goal that is more easily articulated as two sub-goals, A and B. For instance, in the first *Shrek* flick, Shrek's first goal is to get rid of the cartoon characters in his swamp. As he pursues that goal, he discovers another goal, to win Princess Fiona's heart. In this wonderful story, what appears to be the obstacle of Goal A (Princess Fiona) actually becomes the goal for the second half of the movie.

Or, you may discover that what you thought was an obstacle to Goal A was really an obstacle to Goal B. In such a case stop and rethink the goals and objectives right away. It will help to diagram some of these relationships on paper or a whiteboard while someone listens to your explanation and then challenges your thinking. This is one of the benefits of a writing partner. Make sure the obstacles and goals are clear and logical. Don't commit a non sequitur and confuse your audience by trying to force a match with a goal and obstacle that may be related but not logically connected. It won't work.

The main obstacle for the protagonist, of course, will probably be the antagonist, whose goals are diametrically opposed to the protagonist. It's not the point of this book to explain opposing character traits and motivations required for character conflict. Other writers do a fine job of that.[102] At this point it is not necessary to plot out all of the obstacles that the antagonist throws in the protagonist's path or when

---

[102] See Hauge, Horton, Seger, and Vogler.

or how. It is good enough that you have clearly in your mind (and hopefully on paper) the goals of both protagonist and antagonist and that those goals are in a logical and natural opposition. We'll get into the detail plotting in the next step.

Step 8 begins on the next page. This is our last step before you set off to write a detailed treatment or first draft of your screenplay. Because of its importance, it too is presented in some detail. Are you ready? Good! Here we go.

ARC PLOTS AND MAJOR DRAMATIC BEATS 14

THE MAJOR PLOT AND TURNING POINTS

In this *just-in-time* chapter (*it's not part of Step 6*) you will discover how a story's major dramatic beats can be uncovered by identifying the dramatic arcs of the main characters. This will prepare you for Step 7 (in the next chapter) where you will determine the major dramatic beats of your story.

The dramatic arcs of the main characters are formally defined by the Moral Premise which you determined in Step 3. As we've discussed, each main character, in order to achieve a particular physical goal, must first achieve a particular psychological goal. While the goals in the physical realm may appear different from character to character, they must be essentially about the same sort of thing, that is, they are metaphors of the same Moral Premise. If the Moral Premise or theme deals with insecurity, then each of the main characters must struggle with some kind of insecurity, even though the physical goals are much different. Thus, the Moral Premise should be stated generally enough so that it applies and even directs the defeat or success of all the main characters.

A CHARACTER'S DRAMATIC ARC

A character's dramatic arc requires that the character change from some degree of good or bad behavior to a different degree of good or bad behavior. But what is evident in a character's external behavior begins on the inside with the character's internal values and decisions. All outward change is driven by inward change, even though that internal change may not be evident to either the character or the audience. In all cases, remember, the psychological drives the physical.

The internal change is best described as the moral arc. Without this moral change there is no motivation or reason for the outward change. The imperfect protagonist makes an improved outward change only through psychological maturity.

The protagonist doesn't have to end up perfect, or do everything right. In fact, the story will be richer if the protagonist is not perfect and by the movie's end still cannot do everything right. Keep it real and light. But the protagonist does have to change either by making some progress toward the controlling virtue (in a good-feeling movie), or slip backwards toward the controlling vice (in a bad-feeling movie). That change is the protagonist's moral arc that you need to plot out.

CHARACTER ARC PLOTS

To keep this discussion simple I'll stick with the traditional three-act structure, although all of this works just as well for other screenplay structures such as the Purchase Pyramid, Stages of Grief and Change, and the Stages of the Mythic Journey. But for now I assume that the plot for the protagonist will develop in such a way that during Act 1 the protagonist is offered a new "challenge," then rejects it, but in the climax of Act 1 accepts the challenge. I am also assuming that conflict for the protagonist escalates throughout Act 2, until he or she is pushed over the edge in the Act 2 climax. Then, in Act 3, the protagonist fights "to the death" to achieve the goal against all odds in the climax of Act 3.

Knowing that each character has a beginning, middle, and end to their individual stories allows us to plot their behaviors in a very simple, three-point arc — beginning, middle, and end. Plotting their arcs out in advance gives the writer confidence that the overall story will also have a beginning, middle, and end... and indeed be, at the same time, about only one thing because each of these three points relates directly to the one Moral Premise.

In the next chapter you'll be directed to create two sets of Arc Plot tables, one set for the "Good Guys" and one set for the "Bad Guys." (See Tables 9 and 10.) Most successful movies have fewer than eight main characters, and many have only three to five. So this plotting is limited to those characters.

These tables do not articulate the character's every move, but they do give structure to the character's change over the duration of the movie. To complete the table for each character: (1) define how the character behaves in the movie's first half; (2) describe how the character is confronted with the truth of the Moral Premise in the Moment of Grace; and (3) describe how the character behaves in the movie's second half. Identifying these three points gives you behavior targets when you are figuring out the rest of the plot and action.

Good-Guy Arc Plots

A good guy who has a career goal will pursue that goal using an inferior method before the Moment of Grace. After the Moment of Grace he'll pursue the same goal using a more successful method. The inferior method will correspond to the vice side of the Moral Premise, and the successful method will correspond to the virtue side of the Moral Premise.

Table 9 — Good-Guy Arc Plots

All of the character's physical arcs relate to or make a metaphor of the one psychological arc of the Moral Premise: *[Vice] leads to [defeat]; but [virtue] leads to [success].*

A (Character Name)	B Behavior Before (Vice Practiced)	C Change Event (Moment of Grace)	D Behavior After (Virtue Practiced)
Career Goal (describe)	In striving toward a career goal (*character*) practices (*vice*) and experiences (*defeat*).	In the career subplot describe how (*character*) is offered a choice between (*vice*) and (*virtue*) and embraces (*virtue*).	In striving toward a career goal (*character*) practices (*virtue*) and experiences (*success*).
Family Goal (describe)	In striving toward a family goal (*character*) practices (*vice*) and experiences (*defeat*).	In the family/group subplot describe how (*character*) is offered a choice between (*vice*) and (*virtue*) and embraces (*virtue*).	In striving toward a family goal (*character*) practices (*virtue*) and experiences (*success*).
Personal Goal (describe)	In striving toward a personal goal (*character*) practices (*vice*) and experiences (*defeat*).	In the personal subplot describe how (*character*) is offered a choice between (*vice*) and (*virtue*) and embraces (*virtue*).	In striving toward a personal goal (*character*) practices (*virtue*) and experiences (*success*).

Thus, in a good-guy Arc Plots table, for each of the good-guy goals, the first column describes the character's goals. The second column describes how the character strives toward the goals practicing the vice (the old method) and experiencing defeat. The third column describes the Moment of Grace where the character realizes some aspect of the Moral Premise and decides he needs to change his method or behavior. And the fourth column describes how the character strives toward the goals practicing the virtue (a new method) and experiencing success.

Bad-Guy Arc Plots

As you work to complete the Good-Guy tables, you'll want to work in parallel on the Bad-Guy tables.

Table 10 — Bad Guy Arc Plots

All of the character's physical arcs relate to or make a metaphor of the one psychological arc of the Moral Premise: *[Vice] leads to [defeat]; and [greater vice] leads to [greater defeat]*.

A (Character Name)	B Behavior Before (Vice Practiced)	C Change Event (Moment of Grace)	D Behavior After (Greater Vice Practiced)
Career Goal (describe)	In striving toward a career goal (*character*) practices (*vice*) and experiences (*defeat*).	In the career subplot (*character*) is offered a clear choice between (*vice*) and (*virtue*) and embraces (*vice*).	In striving toward a career goal (*character*) practices (*greater vice*) and experiences (*greater defeat*).
Family Goal (describe)	In striving toward a family goal (*character*) practices (*vice*) and experiences (*defeat*).	In the family subplot (*character*) is offered a choice between (*vice*) and (*virtue*) and embraces (*vice*).	In striving toward a family goal (*character*) practices (*greater vice*) and experiences (*greater defeat*).
Personal Goal (describe)	In striving toward a personal goal (*character*) practices (*vice*) and experiences (*defeat*).	In the personal subplot (*character*) is offered a clear choice between (*vice*) and (*virtue*) and embraces (*vice*).	In striving toward a personal goal (*character*) practices (*greater vice*) and experiences (*greater defeat*).

Be aware of how the two tables need to be different. How they are different depends on the kind of antagonist the bad guys are. Chapter I described some of the different kinds of antagonists you might find in a movie. Sometimes the antagonist, like Sergeant Foley in *An Officer and a Gentleman*, is psychologically actually trying to help the protagonist achieve his goals, but physically appears to be doing the opposite. Other times, like Hans Gruber in *Die Hard*, the antagonist would literally like to kill the protagonist. Consequently, there is not a generic form of what the antagonist arc should look like. The only hard-and-fast rules I've been able to come up with are these:

1. The antagonist always creates physical obstacles for the protagonist.

2. The antagonist forces the protagonist to confront the Moral Premise at the Moment of Grace.

3. The Moral Premise is true for all characters, even the antagonist.

Because the antagonist's arc is sometimes hard to pin down, Table II offers an alternative Arc Plot for bad guys.

Table II — Alternate Bad-Guy Arc Plot
All of the character's physical arcs relate to or make a metaphor of the one psychological arc of the Moral Premise: *[Distorted Virtue] leads to [Distorted Success]; but [vice] leads to [defeat].*

(Character Name)	Behavior Before (Distorted Virtue Practiced)	Change Event (Moment of Grace)	Behavior After (Virtue Practiced)
Goal (describe)	In striving toward goal (*character*) practices (*distorted virtue*) and experiences (*distorted success*).	In the subplot (*character*) is offered a clear choice between (*vice*) and (*virtue*) and embraces vice.	In striving toward goal (*character*) practices (*vice*) and experiences (*defeat*).

Here you'll notice that early in the film the antagonist practices a distorted version of the virtue and achieves a distorted version of success. But after the antagonist's Moment of Grace, when the vice is fully embraced, the defeat is inevitable. Table 14 provides specific examples from *The Incredibles* of what we've just looked at in Tables 10 and 11.

General Instructions for Arc Plots

You can be as detailed as you want in each of the Arc Plot tables. But their purpose is to give broad structure to your character's psychological and physical journey, and provide you with clear behavior targets as you flesh out the various incidents in the character's life.

Tables 9-11 provide generic forms of the plotting required, using generic sentences inserted with italicized common nouns that you can replace with specific and proper nouns as they pertain to your story. These generic sentence forms will get you going in the right direction. Comparing the italicized nouns from one cell to another will give you an idea of the kind of mental work you need to do to determine a character's arc. You'll notice that the specific examples in Tables 12-14 do not follow the generic form exactly, but do trace the chance of the character's behavior.

Keep the descriptions in the cells physical and observable by the audience. You need to be describing visible actions, not internal thoughts. The adage at work here is: *Actions speak a thousand words.* You're using words in the table, but you're describing the actions exhibited by the characters. Keep your words visual. As you work to complete Arc Plot tables for your story, you'll have to be patient and put on your critical thinking cap. It's easy to fill in a table cell that sounds right, but the next morning it becomes obvious that you're not describing a physical action or visual behavior, but a mental attitude. Attitudes are okay to begin with, but before you go much further, you must come up with an action the audience can see.

Creating Arc Plot tables for protagonists and antagonists will take some time to finish and polish. But you are establishing the major dramatic beats for all your main characters. Take time to contemplate them, contrasting and comparing the various traits and how they interact with the Moral Premise, and how their vices and virtues change over the course of the story.

MULTIPLE GOALS

One Character, Multiple Goals

The more involved a character is in your story, the better we should know him or her, and the more physical goals the character will need to be well-rounded, intriguing, and dramatic. The different goals can relate to the different aspects of the character's life. Thus, as we discussed in Chapter 5, Bruce Nolan's *career* goal, and the physical spine of the movie, is to become a TV news anchor. His *family* goal is to keep Grace as his girlfriend. His *public* goal is to achieve notoriety. And Bruce's *personal* goal is to housebreak Sam, his dog. Regardless of how many goals a single character may have, remember that they are all metaphors for the goal represented in the movie's Moral Premise. Here in Table 12 is an example of how Bruce's goals can be articulated in an Arc Plots table. Notice how each row visually uses his actions to prove the movie's Moral Premise.

Table 12 — Bruce Nolan's Arc Plot

All of Bruce's physical arcs relate to or make a metaphor of the one psychological arc of the Moral Premise: *Expecting a miracle leads to frustration; but being a miracle leads to peace.*

Character	Behavior Before (Vice Practiced)	Change Event (Moment of Grace)	Behavior After (Virtue Practiced)
BRUCE NOLAN General Goal **To have peace and meaning in his life.**	Bruce expects others (including God) to miraculously labor and do things for him. But even with God's power, Bruce is frustrated.	Bruce realizes that to find peace he's going to have to do things for others with the gifts he's been given, and only when his gifts are not enough can he rely on others to help.	Bruce does things for others. At first his deeds are perfunctory, but later they're out of real compassion. He begins to be the miracle in the lives of others, and he finds peace.
BRUCE NOLAN's Career Goal **To have a meaningful job.**	— Bruce expects to be made anchor without earning it. — Bruce uses God's power to miraculously get the anchor job. — Bruce uses miracles that serve himself not others.	Bruce begins to hear the prayers of everyone around him, but he can do nothing about them. He begins to recognize his limitations (at 45 min.).	— Bruce tries to answer everyone's prayers. — Bruce helps to push a stalled car out of traffic. — Bruce gives the anchor job back to Evan, and sees meaning in using his gifts for doing lighter news stories.
BRUCE NOLAN's Family Goal **To keep Grace around.**	— Bruce refuses to help Grace with picture album. — Bruce yells at Grace to take Sam, his dog, outside. — Bruce uses miracles to give Grace romance, sex, and big boobs.	Bruce tries to use God's power to force Grace to love him. He again recognizes that he can't expect miracles, but has to labor for her love (at 72 min.).	— Bruce labors to court Grace. — Bruce assembles their picture album. — Bruce humbly prays for Grace like she prayed for him.
BRUCE NOLAN's Personal Goal **To housebreak Sam.**	— Bruce "reacts" angrily, asking Grace to take Sam, HIS dog outside. — Bruce "reacts" angrily at Sam for peeing in the apartment.	After hearing prayers for the first time, Bruce orders Sam to use the toilet. Sam never again pees in the house (at 45 min.).	— Bruce proactively, labors to take Sam outside, and to carry out chair for Sam to learn to pee. — Bruce gets Sam to pee on the grass without the chair. Bruce's happy: "We did it."
BRUCE NOLAN's Public Goal **To gain notoriety.**	Bruce takes his angst out on those in the community he's interviewing because they're not helping him to "look" good.	Bruce sees the community pushing over his "Mr. Exclusive" sign (at 76 min.).	Bruce gives joy to the community by being the miracle for them and giving his blood.

Multiple Characters, Multiple Goals

All main characters in your story should have at least one physical goal that relates to the Moral Premise. Here is an example from *The Incredibles* — the story about a family of superheroes in hiding, who struggle to find their way in a world that doesn't want them. There are six main characters, four protagonists and two antagonists. The protagonists are Bob Parr (aka Mr. Incredible, Dad), Helen Parr (aka Elastigirl, Mom), their children Violet (a shy teenager with untested stealth and force field capability), and Dash (an impetuous lad who's very fast on his feet). The family's two antagonists are the general public who have sued the extended family of superheroes into anonymity, thus weakening their ranks, and Syndrome (aka Buddy), a superhero wannabe, whose thirst for fame is exceeded only by his ability to invent monstrous weapons.

The Moral Premise for *The Incredibles* can be stated like this:

> *Battling adversity alone leads to weakness and defeat; but*
> *Battling adversity as a family leads to strength and victory.*

Tables 13 and 14 examine each of the characters and their goals.

Bob Parr/Mr. Incredible wants to be Mr. Incredible again, save people in trouble, and be valued by the public. Helen Parr/Elastigirl wants to have a normal family and meet the needs of Bob and their children, Violet, Dash, and Jack-Jack. Violet wants to have more self-confidence and get Tony to recognize her. Dash wants to participate in school sports (be a sports hero) and gain recognition for his natural gifts. Dash's goal is very similar to his Dad's. And Violet's goal mirrors her Mom's in that Helen works hard to keep Bob's attention on her and the family, and Violet wants similar recognition from Tony.

Buddy Pine/Syndrome wants to be a superhero, but because he doesn't have the required natural gifts he gives himself the goal of destroying all the superheroes with his inventions, so that when no one is super, only he will be left to punch his buttons and pretend to be super.

The Public wants to live in safety.

Table 13 — THE INCREDIBLES Good-Guy Arc Plots

The Moral Premise: *Battling adversity alone leads to weakness and defeat; but battling adversity as a family leads to strength and victory.*

PROTAGONISTS Goals	Behavior Before (Vice Practiced) Character *battles adversary alone* that leads to *weakness* and *defeat*.	Change Event (Moment of Grace) Character is offered clear choice between *battling alone* or *with family*.	Behavior After (Virtue Practiced) Character *battles adversary with family* and experiences *strength* and *victory*.
BOB PARR/ MR. INCREDIBLE To be Mr. Incredible again, save people in trouble, and be valued by the public.	Bob's insistence on "working alone" gets him in increasing trouble, and in fact motivates Buddy Pine to become Syndrome. Bob's secretiveness gets him in trouble with Helen (who thinks he's found a "lover"), and he becomes vulnerable and weak when battling Syndrome's droids. His "nights out" with Frozone playing secret superheroes also plays into the Moral Premise. He only succeeds at the one rescue we see because Frozone, part of his extended family of supers, gives Bob increased strength.	Bob discovers that Syndrome has "terminated" Bob's extended family of superheroes, and he essentially sees himself in the "mirror" also as "terminated." But when his own family shows up to battle with him, he's glad to see them, and later admits he's been a bad father because he's "been so obsessed with being undervalued" that he needed to do things alone to prove his worth.	It takes Bob a while to be fully convinced of what he first began to realize at the Moment of Grace. At 1 hr 36 min., just before the final battle, he admits he's not strong enough, and Helen reminds him that "If we were to work together, you won't have to be... Hey we're superheroes" (we're a family). The entire family AND Frozone work together as a family to defeat Syndrome and the Omnidroid. It's obvious that by himself, Bob would not be able to defeat the Omnidroid or Syndrome.

Table 13 — Continued

HELEN PARR/ ELASTIGIRL			
To have a normal family and meet the needs of Bob and their children.	Helen practices the good side of the Moral Premise most of the way through the movie. But, when the kids are fighting at dinner, Helen is too weak at keeping the family together, until Bob works with her. And when she visits Edna's super-stitch-ery lab, she feels defeated (by another woman) because she failed to be with Bob in his needs.	Edna reminds Helen: "You are Elastigirl! Pull yourself together... What will you do?... You will show him that you remember that he is Mr. Incredible. And you will remind him who YOU are. Now you know where he is. Go. confront him. Fight. WIN!" And Helen goes to battle with her husband... but more importantly she brings super suits for the *whole family.*	She continues to practice and remind Bob that they are stronger when they work together as a family. To protect themselves (and their family) she even reminds her kids, when confronted with danger, to "Use your super powers."
VIOLET PARR			
To have more self-confidence and get Tony to recognize her.	Violet is shy, hides behind her hair, and uses her stealth power to even hide from Tony, a boy that she wishes would notice her. She is weak, and in fact she has trouble at first finding the confidence and strength to use her powers effectively. She even uses her powers to fight with her brother, a use that separates, not unifies, the family. And when she can't figure out how to help her Mom, their jet blows up.	When Helen brings home the super suits from Edna's super-stitchery lab, Violet recognizes the unity and need of her family to be and work together. She finds a babysitter for Jack-Jack, and with Dash she uses her stealthy powers to sneak aboard the jet Helen has chartered to rescue Bob.	Violet practices her power to fight WITH her family to save the world from Syndrome. Most remarkably, she stops hiding behind her hair, and now Tony seems shy with her strengthened confidence. And even after Tony agrees to a date, Violet is quick to join her parents in the bleachers, the source of her real power.
DASH PARR			
To participate in school sports and gain recognition for his natural gifts.	Dash does not have his family's support for a constructive outlet for his powers. They won't let him go out for sports, so he acts alone and puts tacks on the teacher's stool, which weakens his credibility with teacher and parents alike. Well, Bob thinks it's cool that Dash didn't "really" get caught, but that conclusion gets Bob in trouble with Helen.	Dash is ready to help the family when he forces Violet to go along and sneak onto Mom's chartered jet. He's first to put on the family super-suits.	Dash works with his family to save the world from Syndrome. The whole family is nec-essary, working in concert on numer-ous levels. At the end of the movie, Dash gets to run in a school race, with the careful coaching of his parents, he restrains himself from showing off, and maintains his secret identity. And is victorious.

While there isn't a discernible arc for the past and missing super-heroes, it is clear that when the lawsuits came, they could no longer work together as a family. This weakened them to the point that Syndrome was able to "terminate" all of them except for Mr. Incredible, Elastigirl, and Frozone. It is also interesting to point out that because of Bob and Helen's family, and their increased strength at working together, Syndrome was not just prevented from terminating them, but Bob and Helen are on the way to bringing back a larger, stronger family of superheroes through their offspring.

Table 14 will now examine the relationship of the different antagonists' physical goals to the Moral Premise. Both ways of stating the Moral Premise for antagonists are exampled here. Notice that the order of the before and after phrases are swapped from the Buddy Pine/Syndrome arc to the Public arc... but the Moral Premise remains unchanged in meaning.

After you finish studying Table 14 and feel you understand the function and purpose of the arc plot tables, you'll be ready for Step 7, and Chapter 15.

Table 14 — THE INCREDIBLES Bad-Guy Arc Plots

The Moral Premise: *Battling adversity alone leads to weakness and defeat; but battling adversity as a family leads to strength and victory.*

ANTAGONISTS	Behavior Before (Vice Practiced)	Change Event (Moment of Grace)	Behavior After (Virtue Practiced)
Goals	Character *battles adversary as a distorted "family"* and experiences a *distorted strength* and *victory*.	Character is offered clear choice between *battling alone or with family*.	Character *battles adversary alone* that leads to *weakness* and *defeat*.
BUDDY PINE/ SYNDROME To conquer the world, and get even with Mr. Incredible.	Buddy is successful as an enemy to the supers because he's relying on others... represented by his female assistant Mirage, he is able to battle his adversaries (e.g. Mr. Incredible) with increasing strength and success.	When Syndrome is given the opportunity to acknowledge the importance of relying on his "family" (e.g. Mirage) he rejects the idea and shows that he's willing to sacrifice her, to achieve his selfish gains (at 1 hr. 11 min.).	Mirage turns against Syndrome, leaving him alone and weak. Also, when Syndrome is trying to impress the pubic with his "super" powers he can't work with his mechanical family (Omnidroid) very well, and his vulnerability defeats him.
Note difference in structure of arc ➡	Character *battles adversary alone* that leads to *weakness* and *defeat*.	Character is offered clear choice between *battling alone or with family*.	Character *battles adversary as a "family"* and experiences *increased strength* and *victory*.
THE PUBLIC To have a safe society.	When the public tries to go it alone, without their extended family of superheroes, they are weaker and it looks as if they can be easily defeated.	They stand in awe as the supers fight Syndrome and the Omnidroid, but the Moment of Grace comes when the two old men agree that there's "No school like the old school."	The Incredible's government handler congratulates them. After the track meet, when the Underminer shows up, all four of the Incredibles family change identities and prepare to fight, obviously now with the added strength and support of their extended family, the public.

STEP 7.
DETERMINE THE MAJOR DRAMATIC BEATS

15

In this step you will determine the major dramatic beats of your story. This is a big step and will require much contemplation and work. Take a deep breath. There's a lot here.

The goal of this step is to create Arc Tables for your main characters. Create one table, per page, for each main character. At the top of every table for each character write out the same Moral Premise statement — your guide for completing the rest of the table.

Now, pick one character, and on that character's page, in column A (see Table 9 or 10 on pages 123 and 124), list vertically the character's goals (one per row) relating to the different aspects of their life, such as career, family, and personal... or whatever categories make sense for your story. In the heading of column B, identify the generalized vice practiced by this character *before* his or her Moment of Grace, and in column D, identify the virtue practiced *after* the Moment of Grace. Then, in the next three rows, for each of the goals, figure out and write down:

> In column B, the character's vice-ladened behavior trait that leads toward defeat;
> In column C, the event or moment that offers the character a clear choice to change his or her behavior (The Moment of Grace); and
> In column D, the character's virtuous behavior trait that leads the character toward success.

Completing a table like this for each of your main Good-Guy characters will require time and creative thinking. Be aware that you're actually creating the broad sub-plot for each character in different areas of their life. By beginning with a vice, you're giving your Good-Guy character immediate depth and interest; and because the vice is related to the Moral Premise which is related to the physical spine, your whole movie will fit together like sprocket holes in a camera gate.

ARC DEPTHS

Some story arcs and changes in behavior are very slight or shallow, which is not to imply the arc is insignificant. Other arcs show major changes and depth. The longer the chronological story-time, the greater depth you can portray. A story that takes place in one day will typically not show a great change in a character's physical and psychological behavior. Don't overdo it. The criticism assigned justly to many "agenda" films is the result not only of didactic dialogue and images, but also physical and moral arcs that are realistically too deep for the length of the story's timeline.

KEEP IT ABOUT ONE THING

Each of your main characters will have different physical goals, and consequently different physical obstacles. *But each different set of goals and obstacles should be metaphors for the one Moral Premise*. If the physical goals of the various characters do not refer implicitly to the Moral Premise, then you are writing two different movies. Stop. Fix it. A successful movie is about *only one thing*, like a well-constructed sentence or paragraph. Each sentence in a paragraph supports the topic sentence. If it doesn't, get rid of it, use it in a different paragraph, or a different movie.

LATER

After you've finished your Arc Plot tables it's time to use your immense creativity to begin the rough construction of your story's timeline, plot, or sequence of events that will demonstrate the Moral Premise.

Step 8 begins on the next page. This is our last step before you set off to write a detailed treatment or first draft of your screenplay. Because of its importance, it too is presented in some detail. Are you ready? Good! Here we go.

STEP 8.
SEQUENCE THE DRAMATIC BEATS

16

THE PLOT TIMELINE

If you have completed the Arc Plots for seven characters, and each character has three goals (one major, and two minor), you will have described no less than 63 major dramatic beats.[103] That will probably be too much to cram into a 90-minute or even two-hour movie. You might want to consider giving your "lesser" main characters only one goal at first. Regardless, each cell of your Arc Plot tables represents a dramatic beat. You have come a long way in developing your story.

In this final step you're going to make major strides in forming the story's plot by sequencing the dramatic beats suggested by the Arc Plot tables. The task essentially is this: (1) take the contents of each cell of the Arc Plot tables; (2) imagine them as scenes; and (3) place them in a dramatic order that makes an interesting and entertaining story.

While this will not be automatic or linear, it will be exciting as you see your story take form quickly before your eyes. It will require creative and integrated skills; and it will be highly iterative, but almost as soon as you start, magical things will happen as you discover that multiple beats of different characters can come naturally together in a single scene. Yes, it will take time... and time for meditation and relaxation as well. Plan on it. Don't rush the process.

There are, however, some rules that will help you along the way. But to discuss those we first need to give our three-act timeline some labels.

---

[103] 7 (characters) x 3 (goals) x 3 (beginning-middle-ends) = 63 (beats)

Figure 5 (Take 1) - Three-Act Structural Parts

THREE-ACT PARTS

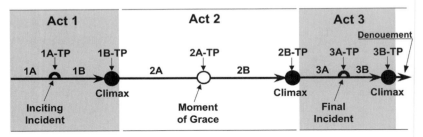

You'll notice in Figure 5 that each act is divided into two parts, labeled 1A and 1B, 2A and 2B, and 3A and 3B. The numbers refer to the three acts, and the "A" refers to the first half of the act, and "B" refers to the second half of the act. At the end of each of these six parts, is a Turning Point (TP) that I call simply 1A-TP, 1B-TP, 2A-TP, etc. The traditional "act breaks" occur just after (or at) 1B-TP, 2B-TP, and 3B-TP, the latter also being the movie's climax. I've used large solid black circles for each act's climax. The inciting incident is at 1A-TP; the Moment of Grace is at 2A-TP (an empty circle), the Final Incident is at 3A-TP, and the dénouement occurs *after* 3B-TP.

BEGINNING, MIDDLE, AND END

The Three-Act structure is a nested group of structures, each in three parts. The movie contains three acts — a beginning (Act 1), a middle (Act 2), and an end (Act 3). Within each act there are also three parts: a beginning (Part A), middle (a Turning Point), and an end (Part B). And in the character's Arc Plots, each character also has their own three-act structure: beginning (Behavior Before), middle (Change Event), and end (Behavior After), with the protagonist's three-act structure coinciding with the movie's three acts.[104]

---

[104] This three-part structure impregnates the whole movie narrative. Each sequence of scenes has a beginning, middle, and an end, as does each scene. Even visual jokes and punch lines are best set up and paid off in groups of threes.

PLOTTING RULES AND DECISIONS

Some of the decisions you need to make about where to place events and scenes from the Arc Plot tables into the timeline may seem obvious. If they are, make those decisions first.

One set of obvious decisions should surround the introduction of your characters. For instance, each character has a cell that describes their Before Behavior trait related to their major goal. For the protagonist this would be the trait linked to the protagonist's major goal, which is the same as the movie's physical spine. That trait needs to be shown in the very first introductory scene of the character in Act 1A. And if it's creatively convenient, all of the traits related to each of the same character's goals should be revealed in 1A, if possible, in that same introductory scene. This can be done with great flair, even without revealing the various goals of the character, although the earlier the goals are introduced to the audience, the more natural the character's motivation from scene to scene will be.

The Before Behavior traits should model closely the introductory description of a character from the screenplay. Thus, by writing the contents of these Before Behavior cells, you're essentially writing the introductory script description for the character.

The next obvious placement of beats in the timeline may be the Change Event for a character's goal. The protagonist's Change Event for their major goal obviously occurs at the movie's Moment of Grace. The Change Events for the other characters are best placed in scenes of their own, so the audience can at least subliminally register the change. I do not recommend that Moments of Grace for different characters be ganged together in the same scene... although there are times when that will work best. The Moment of Grace for secondary characters should probably occur inside of Act 2, but not in Act 1 and not in Act 3. But as we'll see in our capstone example of *Braveheart* (Chapter 17), there are moments of grace in Acts 1 and 3.

This essentially leaves the column labeled Behavior After to be made evident in the scenes following each character's Moment of Grace, especially in Act 3 where the protagonist-like characters are experiencing success and the antagonist-like characters are experiencing defeat. In summary, Act 1 should be reserved for introducing the Behavior Before traits, and Act 3 should be reserved for resolving the Behavior After traits.

VIRTUAL CARD TRICKS

To mechanically facilitate this, use a graphic computer program to create moveable cards on a screen, or pin physical cards on a wall. Each card represents a scene in the movie that, at first, represents at least one dramatic beat.[105]

Here is what I do. I construct my Arc Plot tables in a regular word processing program like Microsoft Word. When I'm ready to start sequencing my dramatic beats I use Appleworks' Drawing program that allows me to create virtual colored index cards on my screen: one card for each scene in the movie. From the Arc Plot tables I copy the text that describes a dramatic beat and then paste it onto the Appleworks card. The Appleworks user interface allows me to easily move cards and text around the screen and reorder scenes and beats for the best dramatic effect.

It would seem that each dramatic beat requires its own card. But as you go along you'll realize that a synergy begins to take over, especially in turning points and climaxes. You'll be delighted to discover how certain scenes lend themselves to containing several dramatic beats from several different characters. Plotting begins to happen naturally and synergistically. When you can combine beats for different characters in a single scene, the sense of story unity will become particularly strong.

To help me keep track of what I'm doing, I'll code the text I copy onto the virtual card so I can trace it back to a particular Arc Plot cell. For instance, if my protagonist is named Lester and he has a family goal, I might code "Lester's Family Goal — Behavior Before" cell as "L-FG-BB." Later on, during the midnight hours when I'm confused about what I'm doing, I can easily trace my work back from the time-line's card display to the Arc Plot tables and Moral Premise.

---

[105] As you flesh out your story and add scenes for transitions, set-ups, and pay-offs, you'll add cards without major dramatic beats, but that is outside the scope of this step and book. In this step, we're only ordering the *major* dramatic beats that critically tie your story and character arcs to the Moral Premise.

BEHAVIOR RAMPS

As your plotting intensifies a character's conflict from the introductory scene toward the Moment of Grace, it will make dramatic sense for the Behavior Before traits to be challenged with greater intensity. Imagine that during Act 2A a character's Behavior Before traits become more difficult for that character to embrace and initiate. This challenge to his practiced vice sets the character up to consider a different method that the Moment of Grace will offer.

In similar fashion, after the Moment of Grace you'll find that it makes dramatic sense for the Behavior After traits to become bolder and bolder as you approach the final climax of the story. Imagine that during Act 3A as a character practices her Behavior After traits they become easier for her; ease gives her the confidence to ultimately succeed in the sequences during and after the Final Incident.

TURNING POINT CHARACTERISTICS

At this point it might be good to recall some important characteristics of turning points that you've learned from other sources.

a. A turning point is when the story heads off in a new direction.

b. Main turning points are the result of decisions made by the protagonist. This decision does not have to be close to the turning point, but the turning point cannot occur without the protagonist's decision and action.

c. All main characters have turning points. While the movie's main story is about the main character, the sub-stories or sub-plots may be about minor characters.

d. Turning points require that a character's mental decisions have physical consequences.

e. Each character must make his or her own decision as to whether to accept or reject the Moral Premise.

f. Sometimes turning points are sharp and other times broad. A sharp turning point occurs when the time between a character's decision and the resulting consequence is short, for example, when the decision has an immediate result. A broad turning point occurs when the time between a character's decision and the resulting consequence is delayed, that is, when the character's decision doesn't have its full impact until scenes later.

SERENDIPITOUS OCCURRENCES

Although the process here in Part II seems very linear and not very open to spontaneous creativity, let me assure you that there is plenty of opportunity for serendipitous occurrences. Fortunately, the converse is also true: there is very little room for ideas that could take the project into wildly creative but unproductive regions. Within the process I've described, the productive, serendipitous occurrences will happen naturally and consistently with what the movie is really about. Using this process I am often surprised at how plot problems get resolved so creatively and quickly because I know how my characters *must* act to be consistent with their own purpose.

THREE-ACT ELEMENT DISCUSSION

As you make progress in sequencing the dramatic beats from the Arc Plot tables, allow me to comment on each of the Three-Act elements and how you might sequence the dramatic beats into a story. Figure 5 is reproduced here for convenience, and for additional help, in Chapter 17 I discuss *Braveheart* as a capstone example.

Figure 5 (Take 2) - Three-Act Structural Parts

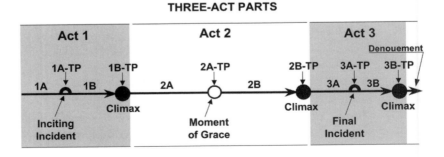

Act 1A

Life before the "new opportunity" or inciting incident. We observe the base line of life for the main characters, the setting, and what their world is like. Establish here the physical and moral process the protagonist uses to make major (and perhaps minor) decisions — i.e., the beginning of the character's moral arc. It might help to remember that everything in a movie is foreshadowed by something earlier in the movie, and quite a lot from Act 1A. I like to think that only in 1A can you introduce entirely new ideas. Everything else that happens is a logical development, consequence, or payoff of something here.

Act 1A's Turning Point — The Inciting Incident

The new opportunity is revealed through the inciting incident. This new opportunity has a clear, definable goal that the protagonist is asked to achieve.

Act 1B

The protagonist rejects the new opportunity and tries to keep his old life and way of doing things intact. But there are forces and obstacles that continue to move him to reconsider and embrace the new opportunity.

Act 1B's Turning Point — Act 1 Climax

The protagonist is forced to accept the new opportunity, and visualizes or articulates a clear physical goal. This becomes the movie's physical spine.

Act 2A

The protagonist tries to make progress toward the new goal using his old moral method, or vice of the Moral Premise statement. Things do not go well. Progress is made, but failure seems to dominate.

Act 2A's Turning Point — the Moment of Grace

Here, grace is offered to the protagonist to change the method of achieving the goal. In terms of the Moral Premise this turning point is the most important, although it can also be the subtlest. It occurs about halfway through the movie. In a good-feeling drama (a comedy), the protagonist embraces the grace and changes her methods to the virtuous side of the Moral Premise formula. In a bad-feeling story (a tragedy), the protagonist rejects the grace and pushes the envelope on the vice side of the Moral Premise formula. The protagonist may not consciously realize what she is doing. But if properly structured, the strong hand of the antagonist will force the protagonist into the new method (or deeper into the old) — and the consequences will be logical and inevitable.

Act 2B

The Protagonist makes solid progress toward the goal using the new method or process — the virtuous side of the Moral Premise formula. But still the protagonist's progress has setbacks that escalate her quest to Act 2's climax.

Act 2B's Turning Point — Act 2 Climax

The Protagonist confronts a major obstacle and burns a major bridge, committing the protagonist forever to the pursuit of the major goal using the new method. There is no turning back.

   This turning point can be incited by a key discovery that shocks and motivates the protagonist even more, shoving her across the bridge and lighting it on fire. Or it can be incited by the wrath of the antagonist. Other times it is the result of the protagonist solving a key part of the mystery that morally or physically commits her to do what comes next. It is the point at which the protagonist finally realizes that progress can indeed be made if a full commitment is made to accept or reject the Moral Premise. It may, in fact, be the place where the protagonist changes from a virtuous defense to a virtuous offense. Or, it may be where the protagonist removes the psychological mask he's been wearing from the beginning of the film and lets others see who he really is.

In the Bedroom's Act 2 climax occurs when Ruth Fowler lies to her husband, Matt, about Richard Strout stalking and smiling at her in town. In that moment, Matt decides to kill Richard and in the next scene he enlists the help of his friend Willis. Matt, in effect, removes the mask of physician and reveals his true nature of killer. Although we don't realize it until the end, it is in this scene where Ruth, too, removes her mask of a teacher-nurturer and reveals who she desires to be, a destroyer.

In *Bruce Almighty*, just when Bruce finally gets his big chance to be the evening news anchor, he walks off the set into the burning streets of Buffalo, forever giving up the news anchor job in order to more fully understand what he needs to know about the Moral Premise.

In *An Officer and a Gentleman* Zack is shoved across the bridge of reliance on friends by Sid's sudden death, and the truth of Zack's arrogant life is shockingly revealed. At once, Zack recognizes that just as Sid, his dad, and his mother all checked out on him — and he hates them for it — he is doing the same thing to Paula.

Act 3A

Now, the setbacks become more threatening, and more physical. Physical and spiritual peril increase by an order of magnitude, and the protagonist does not have a way (physically or psychologically) out of the situation. The protagonist's back is against the wall.

In an action-adventure movie, the Act 2B peril can be small, slow, and involve just a few other characters; but now in Act 3A the peril is large, fast, and involves many characters. In Act 2B the protagonist may be chased by the bad guys, but in Act 3A the protagonist is chased by the cops as well.

Act 3A's Turning Point

The protagonist must face "death" and be willing and ready to embrace it in order to accomplish the goal. His will to sacrifice must be sincere and real. The event here is the "final incident" that propels

146 THE MORAL PREMISE | STANLEY D. WILLIAMS, PH.D.

the story to its climax. It is the bookend to the "inciting incident" of Act 1A's Turning Point.

Act 3B

The protagonist fights to the "death" or success. Pull out all the physical and psychological stops. Demonstrate the protagonist's and antagonist's clever perseverance to the end.

Act 3B's Turning Point — the Movie's Climax

In the end, the protagonist "dies" or succeeds; her goal firmly achieved or utterly lost, while the opposite is true for the antagonist.

Dénouement

Tie together the loose ends, and find a way to state the Moral Premise visually and, if necessary, in succinct dialogue. This is where you can tell the audience what the movie was really all about. For example, at the end of *The Hurricane*, just minutes before the federal judge releases Rubin Carter from prison, Carter says to his young champion, Lesra Martin: "Hate put me in prison. Love's gonna bust me out" (at 2 hr. 14 min.). That line is a near-perfect articulation of the movie's Moral Premise around which every major turning point pivots:

> *Hate leads to imprisonment; but*
> *Love leads to freedom.*

17

As a final example let's examine the Academy Award–winning Best Picture for 1995, *Braveheart* — the story of William Wallace, a commoner of unique passion and skill, who unites Scotland in the 13th century by giving up his life for freedom and sets the stage for Robert the Bruce to rid Scotland of English tyranny. First, we'll determine the movie's Moral Premise. Second, we'll create an Arc Plots table for several of the central characters. And third, we'll identify the main dramatic beats of the story's three-act structure.

BRAVEHEART'S MORAL PREMISE

In deciphering *Braveheart's* Moral Premise there are several strong themes that deserve consideration: (a) the power of love's embrace to loosen the stranglehold of hate; (b) the two contrary and ironic roads to peace — the acceptance of tyranny and its demeaning violation, or the struggle for freedom and its embrace of death; (c) the sources of compromise — greed and treachery — as avoiders of war; and (d) aristocracy's call to use their position to protect the common people.

To zero in on the Moral Premise it will help to examine any recurring motifs or patterns of cause and effect, especially the actions taken by protagonists and antagonists and the resulting consequences. One motif is the continual cowardice of the Scottish nobles as they compromise their country's liberty in exchange for titles, estates, and gold. The result is a cruel oppression of the commoner and an increasingly heavy English tax. But such is the price of peace, reason the nobles, and thus, begrudgingly, they give their allegiance to Longshanks whose predictable response is further enslavement.

Things begin to change, however, when William Wallace secretly marries his childhood friend, Murron. Days later, an English soldier tries to rape her. Wallace helps her fight the soldier off, then puts her on a horse to spirit her away before Wallace too flees into the woods. But, unseen by Wallace, Murron is captured by another soldier and taken to the English magistrate. Angry that a King's soldier has been assaulted, the magistrate takes the opportunity to demonstrate English contempt for the rights of commoners. With disdain he publicly slits Murron's throat, and challenges Wallace to seek revenge. Although Wallace had before refused to entertain rebellion against the English, now he takes up the reigns of leadership — and freedom — Wallace's battle cry to his dying breath.

Midway through the film (at 1 hr. 35 min.) Wallace angrily addresses the Scottish nobles who moments before have knighted him as guardian and high protector of Scotland:

WILLIAM WALLACE

You're so concerned with
squabbling for the scraps from
Longshank's table that you've
missed your God-given right to
something better. There is a
difference between us. You think
the people of this country exist
to provide you with position. I
think your position exists to
provide those people with
freedom. And I go to make sure
that they have it.

This speech summarizes well the two sides of the story's Moral Premise. The vice is the nobles' cowardly compromise encouraged by their greed for position, and the virtue is their divine call to sacrificially provide their people with freedom — something our hero takes up as his own call. What is also evident is that the commoner alone cannot win Scotland's freedom. From the first images of the movie to nearly the last, commoners die with little progress toward true liberty. It is only when the rightful ruler of Scotland, Robert the Bruce, takes up the battle cry for liberty that freedom comes. Therefore, the long form of *Braveheart's* Moral Premise is:

> *The willingness of leaders to compromise liberty leads to tyranny; but*
> *The willingness of leaders to die for liberty leads to freedom.*

Or, to put it succinctly:

> *Compromise of liberty leads to tyranny; but*
> *Dying for liberty leads to freedom.*

BRAVEHEART'S ARC PLOTS

Now let's use those statements of the Moral Premise as the universal truths that describe the characters' arcs, the moments of grace, and the story's major turning points.

But first, let me point out that *Braveheart* offers multiple moments of grace for our protagonist. William Wallace is a classic epic hero who doesn't wait for the middle of Act 2, but rather at the end of Act I seizes the virtue of the Moral Premise and his destiny and never lets go. Consequently, although there are tests of increasing ferocity to turn him back to the vice side of the Moral Premise, our epic hero plunges headlong toward his physical goal. Stories like *Braveheart* combine both dramatic turning points and moments of grace to catapult the story's momentum forward. Wallace's behavior on the vice side of the Moral Premise equation only lasts to the climax of Act I when he is forced to accept the quest. Many other times he is tempted to return to the vice side of the Moral Premise, but he never relents, living up to his marquee billing as an epic hero. I've denoted these characteristics in Table 15, which presents three overlapping and ever-broadening goals for Wallace; and Wallace's temptation to the vice side (the shaded cells). In brief, from the end of Act I to the middle of Act 2 Wallace fights for freedom as a commoner. From the middle of Act 2 to his defeat at Falkirk, Wallace fights for freedom as a knight. From then to his death and beyond, Wallace fights for freedom by winning the hearts and minds of the Scottish nobles represented by Robert the Bruce.

Table 15 — BRAVEHEART Protagonist Arc Plots

The Moral Premise: *The willingness of leaders to compromise liberty leads to tyranny; but the willingness of leaders to die for liberty leads to freedom.*

PROTAGONIST Goals WILLIAM WALLACE	Behavior Before (Vice Practiced)	Change Event (Moment of Grace)	Behavior After (Virtue Practiced)
Act 1 As a commoner: To remove English tyranny and bring freedom to Scotland.	Wallace is willing to compromise his liberty so he can raise a family and farm in peace.	At the end of Act 1: An English magistrate slits Murron's throat and challenges Wallace to seek revenge.	Wallace battles and nearly destroys the dominating presence of English rule on *Scottish soil*.
Act 2 As a knight: To fight for the freedom of Scotland's people and not protect his position.	[Wallace is enticed by his nobles, and King Edward I through Isabella, to compromise and not wage war.]	Midway in Act 2: Wallace is knighted and pledges his new position to win Scotland's freedom.	Wallace wages war on *English soil* and is ready to die.
Act 3 In legend and death: To instill bravery into the hearts of Scottish nobles to use their position to fight for freedom.	[Wallace is enticed to swear allegiance to the King, commit his life to the tower, take a pain killer, or cut short the pain of torture.]	At the end of Act 3: The English court, Isabella, and Wallace's executioner offer him compromises. Isabella even hints that he might one day be her prince when she, who carries his child, rules England.	Wallace dies a hero with *freedom* on his lips, passing on his brave heart to the nobles to win Scotland's freedom.

My purpose in this example, as in all the examples of this book, is not just to analyze the structure of successful films but to illustrate how you can apply a similar structure in your own stories. For that reason, Table 15 gives yet another variation on the Protagonist's arc defined by the Moral Premise. Recall that in *The Incredibles* we saw how four co-protagonists can have four different *personal* goals and one *universal* physical goal, all of which support the one Moral Premise. In *Bruce Almighty* we saw how one protagonist can have different physical goals in different *areas* of his life, all of which support the one Moral Premise. And now in *Braveheart* we see how one protagonist can have the same physical goal in three different *dimensions*, at three different *times* of his life, all of which support the one Moral Premise.

Now, notice in Table 16 how a character like Robert the Bruce can have two sequential arcs with opposing goals (one vice and one virtuous) with the turning point from one to the next marked by a second Moment of Grace.

Table 16 — BRAVEHEART Other Guy Arc Plots

The Moral Premise: *The willingness of leaders to compromise liberty leads to tyranny; but the willingness of leaders to die for liberty leads to freedom.*

Goals Robert the Bruce (and other nobles)	Behavior Before (Vice Practiced)	1st Change Event (Moment of Grace — Moral Premise Rejected)	Behavior After (Greater Vice Practiced)
To bring peace to Scotland. (First Arc — Robert is an antagonist.)	Robert desires peace and entitlement to Scotland's throne at nearly any price. He, along with other nobles, waffle between compromise with Longshanks and fighting Longshank's army on Scottish soil.	Wallace is knighted and the Scottish nobles squabble over their royal lineage. Wallace offers them the moral choice between *position* or *people*. Robert at first accepts the virtue of the Moral Premise but then, under his father's tutelage, rejects it.	Robert betrays Wallace at Falkirk. Wallace is defeated, and Scottish commoners are slaughtered. (same as below left)

(Notice change) ➡	Behavior Before (Vice Practiced)	2nd Change Event (Moment of Grace — Moral Premise Accepted)	Behavior After (Virtue Practiced)
(Second Arc — Robert is a co-protagonist.)	Robert betrays Wallace at Falkirk. Wallace is defeated, and Scottish commoners are slaughtered. (same as above right)	Robert walks the battlefield, amidst grieving wives, and children crying over their dead husbands, fathers, and friends. Robert agonizes over his treasonous and evil decision.	Robert sees in his father's rotting, leprous flesh, his own rotting heart — not a brave heart — and declares to his father: "I will never be on the wrong side again." Robert eventually leads the final battle against Longshanks and wins Scotland's freedom.

Antagonist Goal Longshanks, King Edward I	Behavior Before (Vice Practiced)	Change Event (Moment of Grace — Moral Premise Rejected)	Behavior After (Greater Vice Practiced)
To sustain English tyranny over Scotland.	Grants English nobles land in Scotland and Scottish nobles land in England, making both too greedy to oppose his rule.	Several: — At Stirling, Wallace tells the King's men to leave and ask forgiveness for their rape and pillage of Scotland. — Longshanks receives from Wallace the severed head of York's governor.	Longshanks devalues lives of his army, Isabella, his son, the Irish, and the Scots. In the end, he receives the promise of tyranny waged on his own lineage, as on his deathbed Isabella whispers to him: "Your son will not sit long upon the throne, I swear it." Longshanks dies defeated, while Wallace dies victorious.

BRAVEHEART'S MAJOR DRAMATIC BEATS

Now let's take *Braveheart's* Moral Premise and the Arc Plots and imagine how they are plotted out to describe the major dramatic beats of the story described earlier in Step 8.

Begin digression.

Again, although we are engineering these beats after the fact of *Braveheart's* success, the purpose of this section is to embed in your mind what a successful structure looks like so you'll be able to imbue it into your own work. Theoretically,[106] you will (1) devise a Moral Premise; (2) create Arc Plots; and from the Arc Plots (3) determine the sequence of the major dramatic beats. Thereafter, you can begin your story's detailed treatment by referring to the Arc Plot tables and the major dramatic beats, adding scenes and detail to bridge the story from one major beat, and turning point, to the next.

End digression, and back to *Braveheart's* structure.

As we go through each of the major beats of the three-act structure you may want to refer to Figure 5 which I've reproduced here (yet, again) for your convenience.

Figure 5 (Take 3) - Three-Act Structural Parts

THREE-ACT PARTS

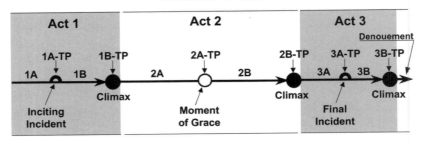

---

106 I use the term "theoretically" advisably. That is, my expectation is that you will determine the major dramatic beats of your story in perhaps a different order or process, but keep in the mind the theory that describes the final result.

Act 1A

Life before the "new opportunity" or inciting incident. We observe the base line of life for the main characters, the setting, and what their world is like to experience.

In *Braveheart*:
Scottish commoners are victimized and murdered by Longshank's English. Young William Wallace wants to fight the English with his father, but is left behind, then left orphaned.

Act 1A's Turning Point — The Inciting Incident

The new opportunity is revealed through the inciting incident. This new opportunity has a clear, definable goal that the protagonist is asked to achieve.

In *Braveheart*:
Adult Wallace witnesses an English noble carry off a young bride as the "noble" claims his "right" of prima noctes — the taking of a commoner bride to his bed on the first night of her marriage.

Act 1B

The protagonist rejects the new opportunity and tries to keep his old life and way of doing things intact. But there are forces and obstacles that continue to move him to reconsider and embrace the new opportunity.

In *Braveheart*:
Wallace woos Murron, but refuses an invitation to a secret meeting of commoners to fight the English. "I came back home to raise crops, and God willing a family. If I can live in peace, I will."

Act 1B's Turning Point — Act 1 Climax

The protagonist is forced to accept the new opportunity, and visualizes or articulates a clear physical goal. This becomes the movie's physical spine.

In *Braveheart*:
Wallace prevents Murron's rape by an English soldier, but she is murdered by the English magistrate. Wallace sets as his goal Scotland's freedom from England.

Act 2A

The protagonist tries to make progress toward the new goal using his old moral method, or vice of the Moral Premise statement. Things do not go well. Progress is made but failure awaits.

In *Braveheart*:
As a commoner Wallace fights the English. But his demise is foreshadowed by the lack of wholehearted support for his leadership by the Scottish nobility who would rather compromise. Note that although Wallace is willing to die for Scotland he's not yet part of its leadership. Although Wallace represents all of Scotland's desire, compromise is alive in the nobles' hearts, and Scotland is still in bondage.

Act 2A's Turning Point — the Moment of Grace

The Moment of Grace is offered the protagonist to change the method of achieving the goal. The offer is considered and embraced although there may be no immediate evidence of the acceptance.

In *Braveheart*:
Wallace is knighted, and is now part of Scottish leadership, whom he must convince to fight alongside him for Scotland's freedom. But treachery is afoot.

Act 2B

The Protagonist makes solid progress toward the goal using the new method or process — the virtuous side of the Moral Premise formula. But still the protagonist's progress has setbacks that escalate his quest to Act 2's climax.

In *Braveheart*:
Wallace attacks and wins at York... on English soil. Wallace is firmly on the virtuous side of the Moral Premise, but he is enticed by Isabella who tempts him with the King's compromise. Yet Scotland as a whole, ruled incognito by Robert the Bruce's leprous father, arranges for compromise.

Act 2B's Turning Point — Act 2 Climax

The Protagonist confronts a major obstacle and burns a major bridge committing the protagonist forever to the pursuit of the major goal using the new method. There is no turning back.

In *Braveheart*:
Wallace is defeated at Falkirk and his army decimated because the Scottish nobles compromised and left Wallace to be slaughtered by the King's army. In another Moment of Grace for Robert, Robert helps Wallace escape capture and certain death.

Act 3A

The setbacks become more threatening, and more physical. Physical and spiritual peril increase by an order of magnitude, and the protagonist does not have a way (physically or psychologically) out of the situation. The protagonist's back is against the wall.

In *Braveheart*:
Wallace's army heals its wounds. Robert rejects his father. Wallace kills Mornay and Lochlan, the turncoat Scottish nobles. Wallace's legacy grows and so does his vulnerability as Longshanks tries to assassinate him. Wallace meets Isabella (her marriage to the prince has not been consummated), and Wallace confirms his love for her and she for him, and in the morning his once commoner bloodline is now royal, through her future child.

Act 3A's Turning Point

The protagonist must face "death" and be willing and ready to embrace it in order to accomplish the goal. His will to sacrifice must be sincere and real. The event here is the "final incident" that propels the story to its climax. It is the bookend to the "inciting incident" of Act 1A's Turning Point.

In *Braveheart*:
Wallace comes to meet Robert the Bruce to unite Scottish forces. Neither knows that Craig, another Scottish noble, has conspired with Robert's leprous father and the English King to capture Wallace. Wallace will now face death, even as Wallace's leadership begins to inspire Robert the Bruce to heroism of his own.

Act 3B
The protagonist fights to the "death" or success. Pull out the physical and psychological stops. Demonstrate the protagonist's and antagonist's clever perseverance to the end.

In *Braveheart*:
Wallace is enticed to confess and find a quick, relatively painless end. Isabella tempts him with love, painkiller, and life in the tower until she can be queen and he her prince. His executioner cannot break Wallace's will even while he is disemboweled.

Act 3B's Turning Point — the Movie's Climax

Death and/or success. Goal firmly achieved and/or utterly lost. In a good-feeling movie the protagonist can achieve success while, at the same time, the antagonist achieves defeat.

In *Braveheart*:
Wallace yells for freedom even during his disembowelment and as he is beheaded. Longshanks dies knowing that his blood will not long sit upon the throne but rather Wallace's. As a leader, Wallace has willingly died for freedom but his bloodline lives on, while the tyrant Longshanks dies in defeat, his bloodline ended.

BRAVEHEART: A CAPSTONE EXAMPLE 157

Dénouement

Tie together the loose ends, and find a way to state the Moral Premise visually and, if necessary, in succinct dialogue. This is where you can tell the audience what the movie was really all about.

In *Braveheart*:
Robert the Bruce, clearly inspired by Wallace, leads a surprise uprising against the English army and wins Scotland's freedom.

PART II: CONCLUSION

Nothing good comes easy. Incorporating a true Moral Premise is not easy, but it is rewarding. Follow the process outlined in Part II for each of your main characters and you'll have your plots and subplots pretty much laid out in story order with every major dramatic beat in place. Beating out the entire timeline will take time. Again, you can't rush it. As you work, take breaks, and make time to contemplate with your right brain how the story should work. If you've done the left-brain work, the right brain will deliver great rewards. And working with a writing partner helps — two left brains and two right brains are better than one of each.

Once you have everything beaten out, write a first draft of a treatment or the screenplay and fill in the details... which of course is no small task. This first draft will practically write itself because you have plotted out every scene and every beat that is needed to give each of your characters depth and direction under the constant guide of the true Moral Premise. I promise, you won't have writer's block. You'll know where things are supposed to start, what needs to happen in the middle, and how it all ends.

In the midst of your writing, if a character wants to go off and do something not in the arc table, or timeline beats, let him... or her. At least for a few days. See what happens. It might be one of those serendipitous occurrences. You'll know soon enough.

You may also have opportunity to consider changing the story in such a way that a minor character seems a lot more interesting, and you'll debate with yourself or your writing partner whether or not to let this minor character become the protagonist. There is nothing wrong with such an excursion. It can be healthy. But, by following the Moral Premise process outlined in this book, you'll be able to quickly evaluate the pros and cons of this new assignment of roles. You may even consider changing the Moral Premise. That's fine as well. The great thing about this process is that, with a little practice, you'll know how to structure the main character arcs, turning points, and climaxes for maximum productivity and potential success.

When you're done you'll have a first draft script that will be several drafts ahead of writing a screenplay just about any other way. For one thing, and a very important thing, your story will be based on a strong, viable, consistently structured, and true Moral Premise that knows where it came from and where it's going.

Congratulations.

Let me know how it goes.

EPILOGUE

You've come a long ways. I hope you feel empowered. I do. I've just been able to share with you one of the most powerful theories about narrative stories, and how you can incorporate it into your own unique tales. Whether you're writing for the big screen, small screen, novel, storybook, or stage, the Moral Premise is the best tool I know of to focus your story structure into a satisfying whole with a promise of success.

There is one more thing I want to leave with you. The Moral Premise can be short-handed with four very simple words:

> *Vanquish Fear,*
> *Bestow Hope.*

Do you see it? Vice leads to fear, virtue leads to hope. Audiences almost universally seek out movies that remove fear and give them hope. That doesn't mean they avoid scary movies, but rather they seek movies that give them hope after the movie is over. Horror movies like *The Ring* or *Alien* do that as well as animated features like *Ice Age* or *The Incredibles.* How? Through the Moral Premise they remind audiences of a universal truth that can make life better.

And that's what the Moral Premise can do for your writing career as well — vanquish fear and bestow hope.

APPENDIX — RESEARCH ABSTRACT

This book can trace its origins to the qualitative and quantitative research I conducted from 1994 to 1998. Below is an abstract of the research (600 pages) available through UMI Dissertation Services. The results showed a strong correlation between the consistency and truth of a Moral Premise in a film and the film's box office success. Because of the small sample size, the conclusions are not statistically significant. Later, informal research, however, confirmed the findings to be significant.

NARRATIVE ARGUMENT VALIDITY AND FILM POPULARITY
STANLEY D. WILLIAMS
December 1998
Wayne State University

Feature film producers continually strive to understand the characteristics of successful filmmaking. This descriptive research examines one of the long claimed elements of successful narrative — the premise and its logical support by the film's individual scenes in order to predict ticket sales.

Just as an informal valid argument uses numerous pieces of evidence leading an audience to a conclusion so a film uses the informal evidence presented in scenes to drive home the validity or truth of the film's narrative Moral Premise. The main research question was: *Is there evidence to suggest that the validity of a film's argument can predict a film's popularity for a defined audience?* A normative ideological continuum of values regarding sexuality, family, money, and authority was established. In each of 12 films, the scenes' central messages and the individual film premises were qualitatively compared to this normative audience to establish each film's validity according to this formula:

Figure 6 - Film Validity Equation

$$V = \left\{ \sum_{x=1}^{x=n} \frac{Vs_x + Vp + Vsp_x}{3} \right\} / n$$

where V is the film's validity, Vs_x is the validity of each individual scene, Vp is the validity of the premise, Vsp_x is a measure of how well the scene supports the premise, and n is the number of scenes defined within a particular film.

Six films and their sequels were chosen to minimize variability. The films analyzed were: *Caddyshack* (1980), *Caddyshack II* (1988), *The Terminator* (1984), *Terminator 2* (1991), *Lethal Weapon* (1987), *Lethal Weapon II* (1989), *Die Hard* (1988), *Die Hard 2* (1990), *City Slickers* (1991), *City Slickers II* (1994), *Father of the Bride* (1991), and *Father of the Bride II* (1995).

The results of the research suggest that the popularity of a film with a defined audience can, to some extent, be predicted by quantitative evaluation of each Scene's Central Message and the Film's Overall [moral] Premise.

Pearson's r correlation coefficient between a film's validity and the tickets sold was calculated for all 12 films at 0.618, for the six action films at 0.474, for the six comedy films at 0.824, and for the eight most modestly attended films at 0.876.

FILMS CITED[107]

Alien (1979). Director: Ridley Scott. Screenplay: Dan O'Bannon. 20th Century Fox Film Corp. (USA DVD).

American Beauty (1999). Director: Sam Mendes. Screenwriter: Alan Ball. Dreamworks (USA DVD).

Armageddon (1998). Director: Michael Bay. Screenwriters: Jonathan Hensleigh & J. J. Abrams. The Criterion Collection (USA DVD).

Batman (1989). Director: Tim Burton. Screenwriter: Sam Hamm & Warren Skaaren. Warner Home Video (USA DVD).

A Beautiful Mind (2001). Director: Ron Howard. Screenwriter: Akiva Goldsman (Novel: Sylvia Nasar). Universal Studios (USA DVD). (Copyright 2001, Universal Studios)

Beverly Hills Cop (1984). Director: Martin Brest. Story: Danilo Bach & Daniel Petrie Jr. Paramount Home video (USA DVD).

Braveheart (1995). Director: Mel Gibson. Screenplay: Randall Wallace. Paramount Home Video (USA DVD). (Copyright 1995, Paramount Home Video)

The Breakfast Club (1985). Director: John Hughes. Screenplay: John Hughes. MCA/Universal Pictures (USA DVD).

Bruce Almighty (2003). Director: Tom Shadyac. Screenplay: Steve Koren, Mark O'Keefe & Steve Oedekerk. Universal Studios (USA DVD). (Copyright 2003, Universal Studios)

Caddyshack (1980). Director: Harold Ramis. Screenplay: Brian Doyle-Murray, Harold Ramis & Douglas Kenney. Warner Home video (USA DVD).

---

[107] Internet Movie Database (*http://www.imdb.com*) and DVD labels. Company name is the US DVD Distributor.

Caddyshack II (1988). Director: Allan Arkush. Screenplay: Harold Ramis & Peter Torokvei. Warner Bros. (USA).

City Slickers (1991). Director: Ron Underwood. Screenplay: Lowell Ganz & Babaloo Mandel. MGM/UA Home Entertainment Inc (USA DVD).

City Slickers II: The Legend of Curly's Gold (1994). Director: Paul Weiland. Screenplay: Lowell Ganz & Babaloo Mandel. Warner Home Video (USA DVD).

Clear and Present Danger (1994). Director: Phillip Noyce. Screenplay: Donald Stewart, Steven Zaillian & John Milius (Novel: Tom Clancy). Paramount Home Video (USA DVD).

Columbo (1971-2003 TV). Creator: Richard Levinson. Universal Television.

The Decalogue (1987). Director: Krzyszto Kieslowski. Screenwriters: Krzyszlof Piesiewicz and Krzyszto Kieslowski. Copyright 1987-1988 Telewizja Polska S.A.; 2003 Facets Multi-Media Inc.

Die Hard (1988). Director: John McTiernan. Screenplay: Jeb Stuart & Steven E. deSouza (Novel: Roderick Thorp, *Nothing Lasts Forever*). 20th Century Fox Film Corp. (USA DVD). (Copyright 1988, 20th Century Fox Home Entertainment)

Die Hard 2 (1990). Director: Renny Harlin. Screenplay: Steven E. deSouza & Doug Richardson (Novel: Walter Wager 58 Minutes). 20th Century Fox Home Entertainment (USA DVD).

Dirty Harry (1971). Director: Don Siegel Screenplay: Harry Julian Fink, Rita M. Fink & Dean Riesner. Warner Home Video (USA DVD).

Father of the Bride (1991). Director: Charles Shyer. Screenplay: Frances Goodrich, Albert Hackett, Nancy Meyers & Charles Shyer. Touchstone Home Video (USA DVD).

Father of the Bride II (1995). Director: Charles Shyer. Screenplay: Frances Goodrich, Albert Hackett, Nancy Meyers & Charles Shyer. Buena Vista Pictures (USA DVD).

Finding Nemo (2003). Director: Andrew Stanton & Lee Unkrich. Screenplay: Andrew Stanton, Bob Peterson & David Reynolds. Walt Disney Pictures (USA DVD).

Fly Away Home (1996). Director: Carroll Ballard. Screenplay: Robert Rodat & Vince McKewin (Autobiography: Bill Lishman). Columbia Pictures (USA DVD).

Galaxy Quest (1999). Director: Dean Parisot. Screenplay: David Howard & Robert Gordon. Dreamworks Home Entertainment (USA DVD).

Gone in 60 Seconds (2000). Director: Dominic Sena. Screenwriter: Scott Rosenberg. Buena Vista Pictures (USA-DVD).

Groundhog Day (1993). Director: Harold Ramis. Screenwriter: Danny Rubin & Harold Ramis. Columbia/Tristar Studios (USA-DVD).

Home Improvement (1991-1999 TV). Created by Carmen Finestra, David McFadzean & Matt Williams. ABC & Buena Vista Television.

The Hurricane (1999). Director: Norman Jewison. Screenplay: Armyan Bernstein & Dan Gordon (Books: Rubin "Hurricane" Carter, *The 16th Round*; Sam Chaiton & Terry Swinton, *Lazarus and the Hurricane*). Touchstone Home Video (USA DVD). (Copyright 2000, Universal Home Video)

Ice Age (2002). Directors: Chris Wedge & Carlos Saldanha. Screenwriters: Michael Berg, Michael J. Wilson & Peter Ackerman. 20th Century Fox Film Corp (USA DVD).

In the Bedroom (2001). Director: Todd Field. Screenplay: Todd Field (Story: Andre Dubus *The Killings*.) Buena Vista Home Video (USA DVD). (Copyright 2001, Miramax Films)

The Incredibles (2004). Director: Brad Bird. Screenplay: Brad Bird. Buena Vista Pictures (USA DVD). (Copyright 2005, Disney/Pixar)

Jaws (1975). Director: Steven Spielberg. Screenplay: Peter Benchley & Carl Gottlieb (Novel: Peter Benchley *Jaws*). Universal Studios Home Video (USA DVD).

Lethal Weapon (1987). Director: Richard Donner. Screenplay: Shane Black. Warner Home Video (USA DVD).

Lethal Weapon II (1989). Director: Richard Donner. Screenplay: Shane Black & Warren Murphy. Warner Home Video (USA DVD).

Levity (2003). Director: Ed Solomon. Screenplay: Ed Solomon. Sony Pictures Classics (USA DVD).

Liar! Liar! (1997). Director: Tom Shadyac. Screenplay: Paul Guay & Stephen Mazur. Universal Pictures (USA DVD). (Copyright 1998, Universal Studios)

Living Dead Girl (2003). Director: Jon Springer. Screenwriter: Jon Springer. Cricket Films.

Love, Actually (2003). Director: Richard Curtis. Screenplay: Richard Curtis. Universal Pictures (USA DVD).

Married with Children (1987-1997 TV). Creators: Ron Leavitt & Michael G. Moye. Fox Network, Columbia TriStar Domestic Television and Sony Pictures Television.

Mars Attacks! (1996). Director: Tim Burton. Writers: Screenwriter: Jonathan Gems (Trading card series: Len Brown et al). Warner Home Video (USA DVD).

Night of the Living Dead (1968). Director: George A. Romero. Screenplay: John A. Russo & George A. Romero. Elite Entertainment & others (USA DVD).

1984 (1985). Director: Michael Radford. Screenplay: Michael Radford (Novel: George Orwell). MGM Home Entertainment.

An Officer and a Gentleman (1982). Director: Taylor Hackford. Screenwriter: Douglas Day Stewart. Paramount Pictures (USA DVD). (Copyright 2000, Paramount Pictures)

Open Water (2003). Director: Chris Kentis. Screenplay: Chris Kentis. Lions Gate Films, Inc. (USA DVD).

Politically Incorrect (1994-2002 TV). Host: Bill Maher. Comedy Central & ABC-TV.

The Prince of Tides (1991). Director: Barbra Streisand. Screenplay: Pat Conroy & Becky Johnston (Novel: Pat Conroy). Columbia Pictures (USA).

Reap the Wild Wind (1942). Director: Cecil B.DeMille. Screenplay: Alan LeMay, Charles Bennett & Jesse Lasky Jr. Universal Studios Home Video (USA DVD).

The Ring (2002). Director: Gore Verbinski. Screenplay: Ehren Kruger (Novel: Koji Suzuki, Ringu). Dreamworks Distribution, LLC (USA DVD).

Schindler's List (1993). Director: Steven Spielberg. Screenplay: Steven Zaillian (Book: Thomas Keneally). MCA/Universal Home Video (USA DVD).

Seinfeld (1990-1998 TV). Creator: Larry David & Jerry Seinfeld. NBC-TV.

7th Heaven (1996-___ TV). Creator: Brenda Hampton. The WB Television Network.

Shrek (2001). Director: Andrew Adamson & Vicky Jenson. Screenplay: Ted Elliott, Terry Rossio, Joe Stillman & Roger S. H. Schulman (Book: William Steig). Dreamworks Home Entertainment (USA DVD).

The Terminator (1984). Director: James Cameron. Screenplay: James Cameron & Gale Anne Hurd (Screenplays: Harlan Ellison *Soldier, Demon with a Glass Hand*). MGM Home Entertainment (USA DVD).

Terminator 2: Judgement Day (1991). Director: James Cameron. Screenplay: James Cameron & William Wisher Jr. Artisan Entertainment (USA DVD). (Copyright 1991, Artisan Home Entertainment)

There's Something About Mary (1998). Director: Bobby Farrelly & Peter Farrelly. Screenplay: Ed Decter, John J. Strauss, Peter Farrelly & Bobby Farrelly. 20th Century Fox Film Corp. (USA DVD).

A Time To Kill (1996). Director: Joel Schumacher. Screenwriter: Akiva Goldsman (Novel: John Grishman). Warner Home Video (USA DVD).

Tootsie (1982). Director: Sydney Pollack. Screenplay: Larry Gelbart. Columbia TriStar (USA DVD).

Touched by an Angel (1994-2003 TV). Creator: John Masius & Martha Williamson. CBS Television.

When Harry Met Sally (1989). Director: Rob Reiner. Screenplay: Nora Ephron. MGM/UA Home Entertainment, Inc (USA DVD).

TEXTS CITED

Aesop. *Aesop's Fables*. Translated by G. F. Townsend. Available
through Project Gutenberg: *www.gutenberg.org/dirs/etext91/aesop11h.htm*.
(Original works written circa 650 B.C.)

Baehr, T. *The Media-Wise Family*.
Colorado Springs: Chariot Victor/Cook Communications, 1998.

Bonnett, James. *Stealing Fire from the Gods*.
Studio City, CA: Michael Wiese Productions, 1999.

Bunyan, John. *Bunyan's Pilgrim's Progress*.
1678. Reprint, Philadelphia: John C. Winston & Co., 1895.

Burch, R.W. *A Concise Introduction to Logic*. 3rd Edition.
Belmont, CA: Wadsworth, 1988.

Buzan, Tony. *Using Both Sides of Our Brain*.
New York: Penguin, 1991.

Campbell, Joseph. *The Hero with a Thousand Faces*.
1949. Reprint, Princeton, NJ: Princeton University Press, 2004.

Clancy, Tom. *Clear and Present Danger*.
New York: Berkley, 1989.

Claxton, Guy. *Hare Brain Tortoise Mind: How Intelligence Increases When
You Think Less*. New York: HarperCollins, 1997.

Conroy, Pat. *The Prince of Tides*.
New York: Bantam, 1986.

Cooper, Dona. *Writing Great Screenplays for Film and TV*.
New York: ARCO Prentice Hall, 1994.

Covey, Stephen R. *The Seven Habits of Highly Effective People*
(Fireside Edition). New York: Simon & Schuster, 1990.

Curran, S., et al. *Moviebuff*. Electronic database.
Los Angeles: Brookfield Communications, 1996.

Damer, T. E. *Attacking Faulty Reasoning*. 3rd edition.
Belmont, CA: Wadsworth, 1995.

Egri, Lajos. *The Art of Dramatic Writing*.
1946. Reprint, New York: Simon & Schuster, 1960.

Field, Syd. *Screenplay: The Foundations of Screenwriting*. 3rd edition.
New York: Dell, 1994.

Fielding, Henry. *The History of Tom Jones*.
1747. Reprint, Oxford: Oxford, 1998.

Fielding, Henry. *Joseph Andrews*.
1742. Reprint, Mineola, NY: Dover, 2001.

Flesch, Rudolf. *The Art of Clear Thinking*.
New York: Barnes and Noble/Harper & Row, 1973.

Franklin, Benjamin. *The Autobiography of Benjamin Franklin*.
1771. Reprint, Roslyn, NY: Walter J. Black, 1941.

Gardner, Martin. *aha! Insight*.
New York: Scientific American/W H. Freeman, 1978.

Greeley, Andrew. *The Catholic Imagination*.
Berkeley: University of California Press, 2000.

Halperin, J. "A Critical Introduction." *The Theory of the Novel: New Essays*. Edited by J. Halperin.
New York: Oxford University Press, 1974.

Harrison, B. *Henry Fielding's Tom Jones: The Novelist as Moral Philosopher*.
London: Sussex University, 1975.

Hauge, Michael. *Writing Screenplays that Sell*.
New York: HarperCollins, 1991.

Horton, Andrew. *Writing the Character Centered Screenplay*.
Berkeley: University of California Press, 1994.

Hunter, Lew. *Screenwriting 434*.
New York: Perigee, 1993.

Hurlbut, J. L. *Story of the Bible*.
1904. Reprint, Grand Rapids: Zondervan, 1974.

Hutton, J. *Aristotle's Poetics*.
Translated by J. Hutton. New York: Norton, 1982.
(Original work written circa 330 BC).

Jonson, B. *The Alchemist*.
1610. Reprint, Woodbury: Barron's Educational Services, 1965.

McKee, Robert. *Story: Substance, Structure, Style, and the Principles of Screenwriting*. New York: HarperCollins, 1997.

Michener, James A. *Writer's Handbook*.
New York: Random House, 1992.

Milton, John. *The Complete Poetry of John Milton*.
Edited by J. Shawcross. Revised edition. Garden City, NY:
Anchor/Doubleday, 1971.

Osborn, Alex. *Applied Imagination*.
New York: Charles Scribner's Sons, 1979.

Plato. *Apology, Crito, Phaedo, Symposium, Republic*.
Translated by B. Jowett, edited by L. Loomis. Roslyn, NY: Walter J.
Black, 1942. (Original work written 380 BC – 370 BC)

Polti, G. *The Thirty-Six Dramatic Situations*.
Translated by L. Ray. 1921. Reprint, Boston: The Writer, 1977.

Ricoeur, Paul. *Time and Narrative*.
Translated by Kathleen McLaughlin and David Pellauer. Chicago:
University of Chicago Press, 1984.

Schatz, Thomas. *Hollywood Genres*.
New York: McGraw-Hill, 1981.

Seger, Linda. *Making a Good Script Great*. 2nd edition.
Hollywood, CA: Samuel French, 1994.

Smith, Hyrum W. *The 10 Natural Laws of Successful Time and Life Management*. New York: Warner Books, 1994.

Tierno, Michael. *Aristotle's Poetics for Screenwriters*.
New York: Hyperion, 2002.

Trottier, David. *The Screenwriter's Bible*. 3rd edition.
Beverly Hills, CA: Silman-James, 1998.

Twyla Tharp. *The Creative Habit: Learn It and Use It for Life*.
New York: Simon & Schuster, 2003.

Vogler, Christopher. *The Writer's Journey*. 2nd edition.
Studio City, CA: Michael Wiese Productions, 1998.

INDEX OF MORAL PREMISES AND THEMES

A BEAUTIFUL MIND

Depending only on others for our well-being leads to impotency; but taking responsibility for our well-being leads to productivity. 70

BRAVEHEART

Compromise of liberty leads to tyranny; but dying for liberty leads to freedom. 149

The willingness of leaders to compromise liberty leads to tyranny; but he willingness of leaders to die for liberty leads to freedom. 149-151

BRUCE ALMIGHTY

Expecting miracles, or others to labor with their gifts on our behalf, leads to frustration, anger, and chaos; but laboring to be the miracle for others using our own gifts for them leads to contentment, happiness, and peace. 72

Expecting a miracle leads to frustration; but being a miracle leads to peace. 72, 127, 128

Be the miracle! 73

CITY SLICKERS

Selfishness leads to sadness and frowns, but selflessness leads to happiness and smiles. 61

A CLEAR AND PRESENT DANGER

Technological might is right. 29

Silence is the greatest passion of all. 29

DIE HARD

Covetous hatred leads to death and destruction, but sacrificial love leads to life and celebration. 61

True love dies hard. 62

A vulnerable man's good triumphs over a vicious man's evil. 62

Slaying the dragon wins the heart of the princess. 62

Perseverance leads to deliverance. 62

Covetous hatred leads to life and celebration, but sacrificial love leads to self-denial and certain death. (FALSE PREMISE) 89

Lajos Egri Illustrations

Ruthless ambition leads to its own destruction. 5

Frugality leads to waste. 8

Generic Examples

Selfishness leads to isolation; but selflessness leads to community. 111

Compassion leads to understanding and peace. 107

Bragging leads to humiliation; but humility leads to honor. 111

Foolishness leads to death; but wisdom leads to life. 111

Unbridled passion leads to risk; reasoned discernment leads to safety. 111

THE HURRICANE

Hate put me in prison; love's gonna to bust me out. 51, 146

IN THE BEDROOM

Ignoring moral instruction leads to death and bitterness, but flaunting moral instruction leads to killing and dread. 76

Watching over a child's well-being leads to health and life, but undermining a child's well-being leads to sickness and death. 77

THE INCREDIBLES

If we were to work together you won't have to be [strong enough by yourself]... Hey we're super heroes [we're a family]. 46, 130

Battling adversity alone leads to weakness and defeat; but battling adversity as a family leads to strength and victory. 129, 130, 133

James Bond Films

The pursuit of power leads to death and defeat; while the pursuit of justice leads to life and success. 96

LEVITY

Truth leads to levity, but deception leads to despair. 53

LIAR! LIAR!

Lying leads to distrust and rejection; but telling the truth leads to trustworthiness and admiration. 78

LIVING DEAD GIRL

Not eating the body of Christ leads to death; but eating the body of Christ leads to life. 114

LOVE, ACTUALLY

The purpose of life is to love, actually. 67

AN OFFICER AND A GENTLEMAN

In order to be better human beings, we must give ourselves honestly to others, but never sacrifice ourselves for others (Hauge). 62

Giving ourselves honestly to others leads to a better life. 63

Arrogance and dishonesty with others leads to despair and a life not worth living, but giving ourselves honestly to others leads to hope and a better life. 64

Deceiving ourselves and others leads to despair and death; but truthfulness to ourselves and others leads to hope and life. 64

Honest friendships and counselors lead to hope and life; but Dishonest friendships and counselors lead to despair and death. 68

THE PRINCE OF TIDES

Love can heal a violent past and make something beautiful out of the ruins. 29

7th HEAVEN

Proper involvement with your children leads to safety and happiness; but not being properly involved with your children leads to danger and unhappiness. 81

TERMINATOR 2

Sacrificial love leads to life; but hatred leads to death. 97

A TIME TO KILL

Faithfulness leads to justice for both the innocent and the guilty. 29

Unjust hatred leads to a just death. 29

Your Writing Career

Vanquish fear, bestow hope. 161

INDEX

Claxton, Guy 60, 104
cleaniness, as virtue 11
Clear and Present Danger 29
cleverness, as virtue 107, 110
climax
    act 1, 143, 153
    act 2, 144, 155
    act 3, 146, 156
code. *See* virtual card tricks
Columbo 34
comedies 14, 68, 69
comic books 31
communist 21
composer(s) xv, xxi
concluding premise 3
confession. *See* Sacrament of Reconciliation
conflict, dramatic xx, xxi, 8, 9, 12-29, 53, 63-64, 81-82, 113, 119,
    122, 141
connection, with audience 93
conscience 22, 49
consequences 21, 29, 35, 49, 50-51, 61, 65, 79, 91, 93, 111, 141,
    147
controlling idea 5, 33, 34
Cooper, Dana 46, 93
Coppola, Francis Ford 54
core values 14
corollaries, natual law of moral premise 50
courage, as virtue 12, 13, 36, 107, 109, 110
Covey, Stephen 103
Creative Habit, The 60
cruelty, as vice 110

honor, as virtue 14, 20, 38, 107, 110, 111
hook, dramatic 67, 117
hope, as virtue 91
Horton, Andrew 41, 46
human condition, the xx, 4, 25, 36, 37
humility, as virtue 11, 14, 107, 110, 111
Hunter, Lew 45
Hurlbut, Rev. Jesse 22
Hurricane, The 146
Hutton, J. 4
hypocrisy, as vice 110

idealism, in storytelling 28
identification 1, 13, 38, 46, 85-95. *See also* Success, box office
identification patterns 90
identification, subliminal 37
identifying values 9
impatience, as vice 110
implicit, dramatic goals xx, 5, 6, 22, 30, 36, 37, 66, 88, 96
imprisonment, as vice 110
imprisonment, as vice in *The Hurricane* 146
In the Bedroom 17, 74-81, 90, 145
inaction, as vice 109
inciting incident 143, 153
Incredibles, The 14, 46, 126, 129, 130, 133, 150, 161
injustice, as vice 110, 113
instinct, story 54-55
integrity, as virtue 93
internal audience identification 85
internal goals, values, dynamics xvi, 8, 39-40, 46-47, 66, 68, 78, 94, 111, 121, 126
invalid argument 20, 28, 94, 95
invisible story 66, 68
Iraq 21, 82
Israel 21
iterative process 105, 137

ABOUT THE AUTHOR

Stan Williams is an award-winning international filmmaker, writer, and instructor with degrees in physics, communication, and film studies. During the past 30 years, he has produced, written, directed, shot, or edited over 400 projects, including live shows for corporate and entertainment clients in the U.S., Canada, and Europe. His critical essays on film, media, and communication have been published in North America and in Europe. Dr. Williams is also a screenwriter and university filmmaking instructor. He can be reached through his website at *www.StanWilliams.com*.